CARDANO IN A NUTSHELL

THE ULTIMATE GUIDE TO INTRODUCE YOU TO
THE WORLD OF CARDANO ADA,
CRYPTOCURRENCY SMART CONTRACTS AND
TO MASTER IT COMPLETELY

SEBASTIAN ANDRES

WB PUBLISHING

CONTENTS

HOW TO USE THE BOOK

How to use the book

First of all I would like to thank you for your trust and for choosing me as your guide to embark on this journey into the world of Cryptocurrencies. This book will help you to understand and master this world with the objective of obtaining an excellent financial education through the comprehension and understanding of Cryptocurrencies. In this book we will go from the most basic to the most advanced.

We understand that entering the world of cryptocurrencies can be tedious and very slow because there is a lot of information that we must understand and assimilate, usually the pioneers in this type of technology are people who have no problem to generate passive income online because they have some basic knowledge of this world that can help them a lot. The purpose of this book is that you can also shorten this path and have the knowledge in time to take advantage of them, as you know the world of cryptocurrencies moves very quickly and you can not waste time.

This technology is here to stay and to give us, the ordinary people, more economic and financial freedom.

In my experience, one of the things that caught my attention when I became interested in cryptocurrencies back in 2011, was the concept of freedom that is related to currencies such as Bitcoin, Monero, Dash, Zcash, etc. where the control of the whole process always goes by hand with the user because of the privacy they provide. Don't worry, you will understand these concepts later on during the development of the book.

In this book I will teach you the different approaches to Cryptocurrencies and the technology behind it: starting from the actual concept of money to the Blockchain, why it works, what is the secret behind it and we will also debunk some myths related to some concepts.

The objective of this book is to teach you to have a more complete and complex notion about Cryptocurrencies, from the most basic concepts such as knowing how everything works, how the pieces fit together, to the most advanced.

I have also taken the time to suggest some resources to get you started on the right foot. Keep in mind that many of these links are affiliate links, so you will receive some discounts and benefits by using the referred link, at no cost to you. So take advantage of it.

I wrote this book not only to inform you about the world of cryptocurrencies but also to motivate you to take that step that is so hard for you and take action, that is why I want to ask you one thing, do not give up throughout this book, follow the advice at your own risk, I promise you that by finishing this book and applying step by step my advice and teachings you will be able to better understand this world and according to your personal actions achieve financial freedom or also support this initiative that gives power to us citizens against the current financial system that is too manipulated and makes a few people rich.

Again, thank you very much for purchasing this book, I hope you enjoy it.

ABOUT ME

Why should you listen to me?

Greetings, my name is Sebastian Andres, I am an entrepreneur, writer and world traveler. I am a cryptocurrency enthusiast since 2011 when I started to get interested in this world. I feel extremely blessed to have been born in this era, and to be able to experience the growth of these technologies such as the internet and cryptocurrencies.

For more than 10 years I have focused on developing several internet businesses, which taught me to develop my own strategies and methods to generate passive income. Cryptocurrencies was one of them and that is how I achieved financial freedom.

The purpose of my books, more specifically of the collection "Cryptocurrency Basics" (in which I bring the most current and reliable information on cryptocurrencies, if you are interested you can look for the other books in this collection, in which we address other cryptos) is to be a source of inspiration for you and generate a change in those who are not satisfied with the established and know that they can give more, that they can generate a positive change in their lives and get to design that lifestyle they want so much.

I am confident that this information will help you to get that final jump start and get into cryptocurrencies in depth.

DISCLAIMER

Important

Investing in financial markets such as cryptocurrencies and other assets can lead to money losses. The purpose of this book is only educational and does not represent an investment advice, for that there are already many professionals in the area that can help you. Proceed with caution, at your own risk and remember, never invest more than you are willing to lose.

By continuing to read this book you accept this Warning.

1

UNDERSTANDING CARDANO IN A DEEPER WAY

From Smart Contracts to Cardano

Cardano follows a subtly different pattern in parallel with other blockchains. Its Blockchain has two layers, a settlement layer and a computational layer. Their first layer was completed and is now highly functional. This allows consumers to send and receive ADA tokens (the name assigned to the service's currency), from one wallet to another. It uses a similar method that Ether employs. Currently, a layer is being planned and developed; its objective is focused on facilitating its users' initiation and proper registration towards smart contracts. Although it bears some resemblance or similarity to the Ethereum blockchain, Cardano enjoys significant primacy over the Ethereum cryptocurrency.

Let's start by highlighting that Cardano results in a much more configurable digital currency, since it is able to generate variants according to the needs of its users at the last stage. Let's look at the situation that occurs in different regions or countries, where there is a diversity of legal regulations that govern the economic and mercantile dynamics. The same intelligent contract is susceptible to be transcribed in such a way that it allows modifications in the style and manner in which all the aspects of information registered in it are filed, processed and consulted, according to its regulatory norms. Considering, therefore, that there is a digital structure unlinked in its layer, an ADA consumer user will be able to continue giving utility to its particular currency, regardless of the place or geographic zone in which it is located, as long as the legislative determinations are fully complied with.

The computational layer also allows the Cardano project team to make changes using smooth forks and without disrupting the ADA or settlement layer. To verify transactions, it uses the proof-of-participation protocol. Those people, better known as users, who wish to be part of the process will be called validators and will be duly committed to make investments for a certain amount in ADA tokens, thus demonstrating their clear interest in being part of the digital ecosystem.

Although ADA offers low fees and instant transactions, the smart contract layer is still under development. This means that it is far from becoming a currency that can be used to purchase products and services on a day-to-day basis. Furthermore, it should be noted that it is not simply trying to be another currency replacement, but a complete smart contract network that allows countries to ensure compliance while providing affordable and convenient means of transferring money to their users.

That's why it may be two to three years before the second layer is completed. Cardano's odds are better than those of other cryptocurrencies and blockchains because it has opted for a scientific approach that involves receiving input from engineers and industry experts. And while the effort may take longer, it won't have the same problems faced by other blockchains or Blockchain in the crypto ecosystem.

Cardano is an open source blockchain project developed in layers to run financial applications used by businesses, consumers and governments globally. It can be used to send and receive digital money, ensuring direct and fast transfers that have been cryptographically secured. The project features a layered development that allows the dedicated team of coders and engineers to easily maintain and update the blockchain with smooth forks. ADA denotes the blockchain's currency token.

Like Ethereum, Cardano aims to acquire the ability to run decentralized applications or dApps in the future. Upon completion of the final process in the ADA settlement layer, an exclusive processing layer will be established by the staff in favor of Smart Contracts that will stably interact with merchant fees and other legal agreements in finance. Unlike other Blockchain projects, it has taken a research-based approach to solving important problems facing today's consumers.

The long-term vision of blockchain and its cryptocurrency aligns the challenges and requirements of both users and regulators, providing them with a way to participate and interact seamlessly. This innovative style of regulatory digitization is likely to bring financial freedom and inclusion to millions of users around the world who currently lack access to financial services due to a wide variety of reasons. On the one hand, the underlying network will bring regulatory efficiency; on the other, the ADA token will ensure fast and affordable money transfer.

We reiterate the importance of recognizing that the Cardano blockchain consists of two main components.

Cardano Settlement Layer (CSL): which acts as a unit of account and is the place where token holders can send and receive ADA instantly with minimal transaction fees.

Cardano Computational Layer (CCL): which is a set of protocols, which is the backbone of the blockchain and helps execute smart contracts, ensure security and compliance, and enable other advanced functions, such as blacklisting and identity recognition.

Cardano's open-source code is written using Haskell, a secure and universally recognized programming language.

Cardano works on a specially designed proof-of-stake (PoS) blockchain protocol for consensus called Ouroboros. This consensus mechanism allows ADA to be sent and received easily and securely at all times, while ensuring the security of smart contracts on the Cardano blockchain. At the same time, as a PoS consensus mechanism, Ouroboros offers rewards to token holders who stake their ADA to the network and help ensure network consensus.

THE OUROBOROS PROCESS is as follows:

- The network randomly selects some nodes for the opportunity to mine new blocks. These nodes are known as slot leaders.
- The block chain is divided into slots, each of which is called an epoch.
- Slot leaders have the ability to mine their specific epoch or sub-partition of an epoch. Any participant who helps to mine an epoch or part of an epoch receives a reward for their services.
- An epoch can be split infinitely. This means that the Cardano blockchain is, in theory, infinitely scalable, making it possible to run as many transactions as necessary without reaching a bottleneck.

THE BIGGEST BENEFIT of Ouroboros is its mathematical security when choosing blockchain validators. Other blockchains claim that they choose block validators randomly, but these claims cannot be verified. Ouroboros, on the other hand, offers a verifiable way to randomly select a validator and ensure that all token holders who bet ADA to the Cardano blockchain have a fair chance of mining a block and receiving the associated reward. This eliminates any need for excessive computational power prevalent in proof-of-work (PoW) blockchain networks and ensures an objectively fair participation model not found in any other PoS blockchain protocol.

Unlike other major cryptocurrencies such as Bitcoin and Ethereum, Cardano has its own wallet for the ADA cryptocurrency. With the Daedalus wallet, users not only get a wallet, but run a full Blockchain node, giving them full control over their funds and the ability to ensure transparency over the Cardano Blockchain.

In addition, Daedalus serves as the only wallet where ADA holders can participate in the Cardano participation system. There is an operational formality within which Cardano acts and it is the PoS Blockchain, expressed already in previous lines; those who are token holders are in the capacity to be benefited with the payment of the well-known rewards thanks to their ADA proceedings or the conformation of betting teams inherent to the well-known Daedalus wallet. This gives Cardano (ADA) holders the opportunity to earn cryptocurrencies while supporting the network.

The Cardano coin can be used as a transfer of value similar to how cash is currently used. Relative to the crypto universe, especially other digital currencies, mainly Ethereum and Bitcoin, it is often very different; against this, ADA has particular utilities that make it stand out.

One of Cardano's core principles is its PoS blockchain protocol, in which ADA is applied to the blockchain to help stakeholder operators successfully verify transactions on the blockchain. This is where Cardano cryptography comes in handy. Those who stake their ADA to the blockchain are rewarded for their efforts with more Cardano cryptocurrency in return. This system of participation helps maintain security throughout the blockchain.

There is also the use of ADA in voting. In Cardano, unlike other Blockchain projects, it is not the miners who vote and decide on changes to the protocol, it is the token holders. Therefore, when a proposal related to modifications and growths to the Cardano Blockchain is presented, those who have tokens in their possession make use of their ADAs and in this peculiar way make themselves felt and express their intentions. Thus, Cardano holders are considered as active participants in this process.

With total guarantee, seen in this transit of ADA, we will see it in the long term, as a useful resource as a catapult in favor of the Smart Contract platform immersed in the Cardano Blockchain. Developers will use ADA to create smart contracts and applications that run on Cardano's secure, decentralized blockchain. Without a native Cardano currency, there would be no way to execute these contracts.

Cardano (ADA), like many other currencies, is a crypto based on decentralized work and transparency of its transactions. It was launched in 2014 by a group of entrepreneurs and programmers. To punctuate, it is convenient to indicate that Cardano is the generic name of the project and ADA is the name of the currency of the service, i.e.; the token.

Cryptocurrencies increasingly emphasize the security provided by multilevel structures. Cardano was born out of academic research and inquiry and has established itself as the first Blockchain project based on a comprehensive philosophy of science. The cryptocurrencies developed and managed by Charles Hoskinson, who led the Ethereum project in the past, seek to maximize the very potential represented by smart contracts.

From the very beginning, the Cardano development team expressed its intention to take into account the regulatory position and thus create a project oriented to care for and protect the interest and convenience of its users and end consumers. This team of developers was trying to find a middle ground between the need for regulation, on the one hand, and the key principles of privacy and decentralization of Blockchain technology, on the other. As mentioned above, Cardano was born in 2014. At that time, the project was a mix of revolutionary ideas and concepts, the result of joint research and teamwork. Its creator, Charles Hoskinson; set himself the great challenge of overcoming the limitations of existing blockchains.

The relationship between Cardano and Ethereum Cardano (ADA) and Ethereum (ETH) are two of the largest Blockchain platforms in the world. They are also rivals with very different goals and fiercely loyal communities.

Given their lofty profiles in the cryptocurrency world, it is only fair to take a walk through the field of the existing relationship between the two cryptocurrencies in a head-to-head showdown.

Cardano (ADA) Overview Cardano (ADA) is a general purpose blockchain focused on creating a highly secure, scalable, peer-reviewed network for cryptocurrency transactions and decentralized applications. Cardano is a decentralized platform with smart contract capabilities.

However, that's where most of the similarities end. While Ethereum allows for the creation of programmable tokenized applications and assets, Cardano is primarily a financial settlement platform that uses its native ADA token as currency.

Peer-reviewed blockchain Over the years, many so-called Ethereum killers have risen through the ranks with violent conversations about the network's performance and cutting-edge consensus algorithms.

Cardano has taken a completely different tack by heavily marketing its science-first approach. Cardano's code base is written in Haskell; a widely used programming language adopted precisely because of how easy it is to audit.

You may remember that Ethereum developers created the Solidity programming language. It is highly specialized and few developers are experts at writing it, let alone reviewing Solidity code. Why is peer review important? Because the more developers who can review and audit code, the more airtight and secure that code is likely to be. The point is that Cardano developers want the blockchain to be as free of coding flaws as possible to mitigate potential security issues in the future.

Dual-layer design Cardano uses a dual-layer design in its protocol that separates computations from settlements.

It is useful to think of Ethereum, a single-layer protocol that performs computations (smart contracts) and settlements (token transfers) together. Ethereum often gets bogged down by the volume of computational and payment transactions that plague Ethereum miners, resulting in high gas prices.

In contrast, Cardano's separate layers allow smart contracts and decentralized applications to exist independently of ADA token transactions. This separation should allow Cardano to scale, remain economical for developers and users, and inter-operate with other platforms.

Focused on energy efficiency Cardano uses a lightweight proof-of-stake consensus algorithm called Ouroboros, the name of an ancient circular symbol representing a snake biting its tail. The reference is clever because Cardano's proof-of-stake design efficiently uses network resources in a closed-loop system.

Ouroboros works by allowing ADA holders using one of several Cardano wallets, such as Daedlus, to delegate their tokens to validators that keep the network secure. The process requires much less computationally intensive demands, which keeps energy costs very low for running the network.

Recently, Cardano has begun to tout its strength as a more environmentally friendly blockchain than Ethereum. Charles Hoskinson estimates Cardano's energy usage to be a mere 0.01% of Bitcoin's 110.53 TWh.

ADA is the native cryptocurrency token of the Cardano blockchain.

Remember that Cardano is first and foremost a platform for decentralized transactions using the ADA coin. So don't expect flashy use cases and utility from the ADA token; for the most part, it's just decentralized cash with participation enabled.

Using ADA as money ADA tokens exist in a separate transaction layer within the Cardano blockchain. This makes sending and receiving ADA tokens a fast and inexpensive experience as well.

Anyone who has been hit with crazy fees for Ethereum gas will appreciate ADA's inexpensive transactions.

Given Cardano's focus on creating decentralized financial solutions for developing countries, ADA is designed as a near-instantaneous medium of exchange capable of becoming a global currency.

Betting on ADA for passive income Cardano is updated in eras named after revolutionary historical figures. The network is currently in the Shelley era, but is being carefully incorporated into the Goguen update.

In Goguen, Cardano smart contracts will finally be enabled on the main Cardano network. This upgrade will bring Cardano's computational capabilities and use cases up a notch; for reference, Ethereum has had live smart contracts since its launch in 2015. What does any of this have to do with earning passive income with ADA tokens? An increase in Cardano network activity due to the implementation of smart contracts will mean more work for validators. This, in turn, means greater use of wagered ADA tokens and potentially higher wagering rewards.

Enthusiasm for Goguen smart contracts is growing rapidly. Cardano has initialized the Alonzo test network, an early-stage version of smart contracts. However, despite the initial testing phase, ADA holders have wagered more than an additional US$30 million on ADAs.

Betting on ADA is much easier compared to Ethereum 2.0. You don't need to lock the wagered ADA tokens; you can unlock ADA tokens whenever you want.

CARDANO PROS:

- Environmentally friendly design using proof of stake consensus.
- ADA staking does not require token locking
- Dual-layer architecture is fast, scalable and secure

- Cardano is already gaining traction with supply chain use cases
- Focus on developing nations holds promise for future growth

CONS OF CARDANO:

- Too slow to implement industry standard capabilities - Few, if any, widely adopted decentralized applications.
- ADA has gained little traction as a currency
- Hoskinson is a polarizing figure interested in getting attention.
- Cardano has a reputation for being a ghost chain

ETHEREUM (ETH) Overview

Ethereum (ETH) is a smart contract blockchain platform created by an all-star staff of cryptographers in 2015. Today, Ethereum is primarily used to create and host decentralized financial applications and stable currencies.

The most significant contribution Ethereum has made to Blockchain is the invention of smart contracts. Without further ado, let's review what Ethereum smart contracts are and why they are important.

Ethereum Smart Contracts It has been more than a decade since Bitcoin unleashed Blockchain technology on the world. However, few understand that Bitcoin is programmable cash, but technologically it is capable of little else.

Ethereum's founders and lead developers, Vitalik Buterin and Gavin Wood, devised smart contracts to expand Blockchain's utility beyond cash. Smart contracts allow blockchains to behave like powerful decentralized virtual computers, a far cry from simple money as we know it.

What are smart contracts?

Smart contracts, or smart contracts, are basic, lightweight computer programs that run on the Ethereum blockchain. Anyone can build a smart contract containing specific rules performed autonomously. This is how Ethereum applications operate without intermediaries: smart contracts run reliably without anyone operating them.

If you still have difficulty understanding smart contracts, think of them as digital vending machines.

When you go for a soda at a vending machine, you enter an amount of cash and select a soda. Once these two required inputs are made, the vending machine drops the soda and perhaps some change. So, just like a vending machine, a smart contract operates based on pre-programmed inputs (X, Y and Z) to deliver specific outputs (A, B and C).

Before vending machines, someone had to physically sell refreshments. But after their arrival, the machine and its code take care of the job. Smart contracts do the same for any contractual situation that requires trust between two or more parties. Instead of requiring someone to be trusted, smart contracts replace trust by making it implicit in the transaction.

Transitioning from Ethereum 1.0 to Ethereum 2.0 Smart contracts allow anyone to easily create applications on Ethereum that, in theory, can run forever without being censored. Despite the revolutionary nature of this proposal, in practice, Ethereum's potential is hampered by its proof-of-work consensus algorithm.

When Ethereum's developers originally built the network, they borrowed Bitcoin's proof-of-work model. PoW had already proven to be stable, secure and sufficiently decentralized.

The early days of crypto saw far fewer users and transactions. The relatively low network volume meant it was easy for a PoW blockchain like Ethereum to keep up with activity. But as cryptocurrency entered the mainstream with NFT and DeFi applications running on Ethereum, the network's inability to scale became painfully apparent.

PoW consensus works by having miners validate transactions. This keeps the network secure by ensuring that every transaction is honest. The problem is that each miner, or node, processes every transaction on the network. Depending on traffic, some days can see over 500k transactions despite Ethereum's paper speeds of 15 transactions per second.

To combat this problem and make Ethereum much more robust and scalable, developers are implementing Ethereum 2.0. The switch to ETH 2.0 moves the network from proof-of-work to proof-of-stake consensus and introduces fragmentation.

PoS consensus requires much less energy and computing resources, while fragmentation allows validators to verify only transactions in a specific part of the network rather than its entirety.

By the time ETH 2.0 is complete, it should have much higher TPS performance than its current state. That means Ethereum will truly be ready to serve billions of people as a global computer.

Like many, many people, we are sure you're wondering when ETH 2.0 will launch by. In early 2021, Ethereum launched Phase 0 with its beacon chain, but the full launch isn't expected until sometime between 2022 and 2023.

ETH TOKEN EXPLAINED

ETH is the Ethereum cryptocurrency token that powers network transactions. Unlike pure-currency coins like Bitcoin, ETH has a token utility that goes far beyond money.

ETH powers Ethereum transactions Every time a smart contract executes a command, it simultaneously triggers a transaction. In addition to the countless smart contract transactions that occur, there are also the obvious transactions where one Ethereum user sends tokens to another.

Ethereum averages over 1M transactions per day, but even more

impressive is the historical total of over 1000M Ethereum transactions.

All Ethereum transactions run on gas, just like your car. The
difference is that your car uses fossil fuels and Ethereum transactions use ETH tokens. Any wallet that initiates a transaction, whether
to execute smart contracts or send stable coins, must first pay a
gas fee.

Paying network transaction fees is the largest use case for the
ETH token. Ethereum miners receive gas fees to compensate them for
their work in validating the network.

Using ETH as collateral in DeFi.

The power of ETH goes beyond paying for network transactions
and rewarding miners. Because most decentralized financial
applications run on Ethereum, ETH tokens have reserve currency
status in most liquidity pools.

Uniswap is a great example. As the world's largest decentralized
exchange, it processes billions of dollars worth of transactions with
ETH as the base token for most pairs.

Beyond Uniswap, users mint stable coins with cryptographic
collateral such as DAI by depositing ETH as collateral with Maker-
DAO. After getting your hands on tokens from the DAI or Uniswap
liquidity pool, you can deposit them into DeFi vaults by Yearn
Finance for additional interest yield.

Earning ETH participation rewards.

The transition to Ethereum 2.0 brings ETH participation to the
network. Ethereum stake is exciting for everyone because it is profitable, earns interest for wagering ETH, and improves network
performance.

Although ETH 2.0 has not been fully implemented, which is not
expected until at least 2022, the Phase 0 update in January gave the
green light to ETH participation. Rewards are decent on the best

ETH betting pools, but are subject to change, as possibly increasing, as time goes on.

ETHEREUM PROS:

- The industry's largest smart contract Blockchain platform.
- Ethereum is the undisputed home of DeFi and NFT.
- Pioneer traction has locked down tons of mindshare from developers
- Hosts all of Crypto's most widely used decentralized applications.
- Imminent ETH 2.0 upgrade boosts network performance

ETHEREUM CONS:

- Current speed limits result in frequent network congestion
- Ethereum's tariffs are often prohibitively high for developers
- High gas tariffs make DEX and DeFi transactions expensive
- Ethereum development is often disorganized and slow
- ETH 1.0 uses PoW and contributes to climate change

Cardano and smart contracts

At the basic level, Cardano smart contracts will function similarly to those on the Ethereum blockchain. They act as executable programs that are produced on the Cardano blockchain.

Smart contracts will act as digital agreements or guarantees between two parties. Outputs or transactions are only executed when preconditions or inputs are met. Once the conditions are met, the transaction is automatically established. These transactions and their details will stay on the Cardano blockchain forever.

One of the touted advantages about smart contract integration is the lack of people or intermediaries needed to carry out or maintain the contracts, as with traditional agreements. These elements can often slow down the process.

Contract details remain on a decentralized blockchain. This means that agreements are free from risk of manipulation or evasion by third parties, along with greater transparency and traceability.

The inability to change smart contracts carries some risks. If the smart contract includes errors, it may be difficult to change them. Contracts also run the risk of exploiting loopholes. Of course, these are not unique to smart contracts, but transfer a greater burden to programmers rather than, for example, lawyers.

Cardano's smart contract language

Cardano smart contract programmers use one of three languages - Plutus, Marlowe or Glow.

As described by IOHK, Plutus is "a specially designed smart contract execution and development platform that runs both on-chain and off-chain."

Marlowe is Cardano's domain-specific language (DSL) that is most commonly used for financial contracts, while Glow is a DSL used for writing decentralized applications (dApps).

Plutus and Marlowe are powered by Haskell, a functional, research-driven programming language with a foundation in academia and industry. This has given the language a reputation for code robustness and reliability, which could help avoid the vulnerabilities and risks of smart contracts.

Examples of Cardano smart contracts

The hard fork of Alonzo has not yet gone live, which means that no smart contracts are currently running on the Cardano main net.

However, IOHK has launched Marlowe Playground, a browser-based editor for potential Marlowe smart contracts. The Marlowe Playground includes several examples of smart contracts that provide some ideas for possible financial uses, such as escrow contracts, loans and basic swaps.

IOHK also launched Plutus Playground with its own examples. These include smart contracts for a game, a vesting scheme, and a crowdfunding attempt.

There are countless other potential uses for smart contracts, whether for financial transactions, insurance, voting or even digital ID cards.

We will see more when the Alonzo test network goes live on September 1, followed by the main network launch on September 12, 2021.

CARDANO AND SMART Contracts

Cardano has taken a slow and steady approach to its development. The team believes in thorough research and testing before implementation. It may come as a surprise to learn that this is not the norm in cryptocurrencies: in the race to take full advantage of Blockchain technology, many coins first launch products and then improve them as they go along.

In the long run, Cardano's approach will likely result in a more secure, scalable and robust product. Hoskinson designed the blockchain from the ground up to address some of the problems faced by pioneering Bitcoin (BTC) and Ethereum (ETH).

In the short term, it means that other platforms, especially Ethereum, have taken over the lion's share of the market. According to State of the dApps, which tracks decentralized apps; almost 80% of dApps are currently based on Ethereum.

However, Ethereum is struggling because its platform is not fast enough to cope with the high demand. Until it can upgrade to ETH2, users have to deal with high fees and network congestion. Cardano's smart contracts may mean that some of those users will switch to its system.

Why are smart contracts so important?

Smart Contracts are small pieces of code that live on the blockchain. They are game changers. Without them, a Blockchain database is a sophisticated ledger that can record and track transactions and data. But with smart contracts, Blockchain becomes a programmable platform that can host other applications.

Cardano's Alonzo upgrade includes its own smart contract development language called Plutus. Cardano wants people who don't necessarily have a technical background to be able to create smart contracts.

HERE ARE **a few things that smart contracts make possible:**

- Decentralized Finance Applications (DeFi): this is a general term for financial applications that work without intermediaries like banks, for example, that offer loans that don't require a middleman.
- Non-fungible tokens (NFT): these unique digital assets are often collectibles such as art or sports cards, with embedded digital signatures containing ownership information.
- Gaming applications: players can own in-game assets through NFTs, and smart contracts can also change the way gaming economies work.

Getting to know Charles Hoskinson a bit. Founder of Cardano

Charles Hoskinson was born in Hawaii on November 5, 1987. Between 2008 and 2010, he studied Analytic Number Theory at Metropolitan

State University of Denver and the University of Colorado Boulder. Charles is a mathematician, technologist, entrepreneur, developer, chess player and fisherman. He currently works as a mathematician and cryptographic engineer.

Although there are not many details about his childhood, certain blogs, articles and various publications define Charles Hoskinson as an intelligent, efficient and very bright child and teenager with a marked interest in everything related to calculations and numerical operations. As a university student, he studied mathematics and cryptography. Some portals and disclosures describe that his performance in these areas definitely became his true passion.

In 2013 he established, together with a disciplinary staff, the Cryptocurrency Research Group. Between the years 2013 and 2014 he becomes Co-Founder and CEO of Ethereum, together with Vitalik Buterin. Likewise, Charles is CEO and founder of Input Output Hong Kong IOHK in 2015. Hoskinson is one of the lead developers of the Cardano project, launched in 2017. His experience has given him by then, the opportunity to be the founder in addition to Invictus Innovations; in addition to holding important, prominent and outstanding positions for private and public sector companies. It is worth mentioning that Charles was the founding chairman of the Education Committee of the Bitcoin Education Project.

His current goals include education on specialized cryptocurrency topics, evangelization of decentralization and making cryptographic tools an easy and user-friendly resource for the entire crypto ecosystem.

Unlike many other players and prominent industry participants, Charles Hoskinson's entry into the crypto and digital currency ecosystem was much more personal when he was on the board of a company co-founded with developer Dan Larimer, better known as Invictus. Innovations Inc, with which they launched the first platform to develop a decentralized autonomous business, known as BitShares.

This work, or project, opened the first access to what many today know as DAO (acronym for a decentralized autonomous organization), whose direction and management was dictated by a protocol rather than a hierarchical tree of leadership positions.

Later, in 2013, Hoskinson started the Bitcoin Education Project / Cryptocurrency Research Group, which he recorded in one of his first posts on the BitcoinTalk.org forum, informing interested parties that the initiative was completely free to get started.

It was then that he had the opportunity to meet Vitalik Buterin, which paved the way for him to be part of the original group of nine developers who are helping to shape the Ethereum project.

2

CARDANO DEVELOPMENT AND ROADMAP

C ardano is a cryptographic project like no other, characterized by its own operational and functional conditions that make it not only interesting, but also very attractive for the crypto environment and its penetration in the market; capturing day by day more and more interest. Its development process is unprecedented, genuine and sustains its originality, going against most of the rest of the other cryptocurrencies.

One of the strong and fundamental pillars of Cardano is its Roadmap, this being one of the clearest. Currently, the Cardano Blockchain is in the Shelley phase, activated as of June 2020. This upgrade resulted in a frank and excellent improvement in its network decentralization and optimized the scalability of Ouroboros Praos. With this increased decentralization, the network has undoubtedly become more secure, faster, more stable and more scalable.

As we already know and are clear, the Cardano project was founded by Charles Hoskinson, one of those who in turn was a co-founder of Ethereum. This character presented, during the introduction of the project, the goal of Cardano, which is before, in his words, all to learn from the mistakes of Ethereum that encounters significant blockages in scalability, performance and governance issues.

Cardano defines itself as a "non-profit and independent organization", with its main headquarters in Switzerland, the place from where it oversees its growth, progress and development. The Cardano Foundation recognizes itself as the legal custodian of the Cardano brand, which works in conjunction with IOHK and EMURGO to ensure that Cardano is deployed, developed and promoted as a new, safe, clear and committed solution tool to bring about positive global change.

The Cardano Foundation sets its direction for decentralized economic empowerment, working with regulators in different competencies thus shaping Blockchain legislation and trading standards, and consolidating the Cardano community to leverage the Cardano protocol, being of great use in solving real life problems and conflicts, beyond the network.

Within the framework of Cardano's own development, we meet:

Goguen:

The Expansion of Smart Contracts Today, work is underway to include smart contracts within the blockchain. What Goguen is going to do is to add the necessary capability to Cardano so that DAps can be developed on its own Blockchain using the Plutus programming language, a Haskell-based programming language. Currently, the first smart contracts are already running and successfully delivering the expected result, within Alonzo; Cardano's test network. Recall that a test net, is a copy of the blockchain that is mined locally for testing. This takes for granted and assured that any potential failure of the upgrade or update under test does not affect the main network at all.

BASHO:

And general improvements the second Cardano upgrade is known by the name of Basho and has as its basic and fundamental objective, the optimization of the platform. The primary objective of this update is to improve, in its greatest expression, the interoperability and the inclusion of sidechains, which allow to offer the services of this Blockchain in a more perfected way and in improvement of its capabilities.

Thanks to the Basho upgrade, Cardano is expected to become the Blockchain with the highest and highest performance, resilience and flexibility within the cryptocurrency field and ecosystem. Basho should offer the opportunity to develop and incorporate new functionalities in a sustainable and secure way without compromising the security and full trust provided by the network.

VOLTAIR: On-Chain Governance

For the time being the development path concludes with the progress of governance within the Blockchain itself and enhances the decentralization achieved with Shelley. It also strives to achieve self-sufficiency in its development.

Voltair's intention or purpose is to give rise to an On-Chain governance system, with a guaranteed and decentralized treasury system. This mechanism is intended for the long-term financing and healthy development of the project as such. IOHK will cease to be the power or economic force of Cardano at this point, thus giving the project complete and total freedom; in this way the community will bring help and support to the very progress of the improvements proposed by the various development groups.

With total certainty, the great stronghold of Cardano is that its development is driven by an outstanding and recognized team of professionals in the industry, who have been constantly trained in different fields and areas that positively impact the foundations of Cardano's constitution. Its timely development is currently very well focused, always taking into consideration and as a number one quota; the objective is to give everything back to the community. Once its development is fully approved, the community will undoubtedly support and finance the suggestions for improvement that are considered timely and necessary.

Cardano's intention is to develop a truly alternative smart contract management platform that creates a much richer, consistent and effective DeFi ecosystem. All this without racing and without haste, with a proper review of its code in order to avoid those potential security breaches that put the network at risk and in adverse conditions, usually occur.

WHO IS BEHIND CARDANO?

Cardano is a big project, governed by different organizations. This is what its governance looks like.

At the helm of the Cardano project is the Cardano Foundation, a non-profit, not-for-profit entity. Based in Switzerland, the Cardano Foundation achieved an Initial Coin Offering (ICO) of 62.2 million US dollars in the month of October 2015.

Frederik Gregaard, CEO of the Cardano Foundation at present, is a former CFO of PwC Price waterhouse Cooper, one of the big four largest accounting audit firms in the world, alongside KPMG, Deloitte and Ernst & Young. Gregaard says he is currently pursuing a strategy that is applicable and sustainable for the next 50 to 100 years or so.

The Cardano Foundation has set itself an interesting project based on sustainable objectives, supported by pillars of weight and value, focused on five very important management tasks that make

Cardano and its foundation a plan with significant intentions and objectives, inspiring respect and trust.

LET'S see below its main missions:

- As a basic and fundamental aspect: Drive the adoption of Cardano.
- Implement legislation to make Cardano interoperable with various legal and commercial standards.
- Promote, support and grow the Cardano community.
- Secure the self-interest of Cardano's shareholders, ADA holders.
- Facilitate and provide partnerships with the industry world.

To GIVE FULL COMPLIANCE, support and feasibility to these aspects in favor of its development, the Cardano Foundation has formed and maintains an excellent and attractive work team, made up of:

- 5 board members.
- 13 IT specialists (Technical Integrations).
- 4 PR (Public Relationships).
- 3 marketers.
- 5 community managers.

THE DEVELOPMENT of a blockchain as ambitious as Cardano and at the level it was intended to be given and imbued with so much effort and true commitment, is definitely a very painstaking task and complicated enough, so that, up to this point, there is no one who has achieved such a feat, not even in the computational realms of Bitcoin or Ethereum.

It was to the IHK organization, a company created by Charles Hoskinson who was assigned this fascinating project. Hoskinson is part of the multidisciplinary team of 7 developers in charge of founding Ethereum in 2015, and is also one of the two co-founders of the Cardano project. But for a Rockstar-type developer, it is not enough to carry the full load of developing Cardano, so he thought it appropriate to give himself a "little" support.

Input Output Hong Kong - IOHK, one of the most recognized companies nowadays for giving impulse to the creation, offering its support and global support to the Cardano network; one of the most pondered Blockchain projects of the cryptographic present time. IOHK provides software development and technological support to Cardano. It was founded in 2015 in the city of Hong Kong (China), by Charles Hoskinson and Jeremy Wood. Although IOHK, is aimed at companies and is responsible for offering products and services to organizations around the world, it is dedicated exclusively to the development and evolution of Cardano. It is therefore a company dedicated to the development of Blockchain and crypto solutions.

Better known as IOHK, it was conceived under the premise of making, due and optimal use of Blockchain technology in favor of the improvement of P2P solutions, especially aimed at people excluded from the financial services sector. For IOHK, Cardano is the jewel in the crown.

According to the data provided on the Input Output Hong Kong - IOHK website, the company is made up of 256 people who make up its working staff and who are distributed in various regions of the world, who are mostly developers specialized in Blockchain, whose main conformation has the presence of:

- 2 founders
- 5 directors

- More than 30 researchers
- More than 120 engineers
- 10 salespeople

UNLIKE THE VAST majority of blockchains based and founded on technical and/or specialized papers, Cardano is a project with strong academic roots that takes its approach very seriously in favor of growth developments, which are based on research, which has been funded but also published by IOHK , for peer review. Before the implementation of the protocols, it is necessary to go through this critical-objective review and assessment phase, which is unavoidable in order to detect flaws in the protocols.

The default language of the Cardano platform is Haskell, a language that allows mathematical proofs at the level of software performance requirements. In the Cardano Blockchain, the level of security is highly tested and guaranteed.

Despite its thorough, cautious and therefore necessarily slower approach; the IOHK team is not inactive, let alone passive towards Cardano, as this is the project that has seen the most activity on Github throughout 2019, well ahead of Ethereum.

Emurgo: Cardano's trading arm.

Emurgo is the trading arm of Cardano. The digital investment company is in charge of building bridges between Blockchain and the economic world: states, companies and individuals among others. Emurgo markets everything related and concerning industrial solutions based on blockchain. Highlighting among them:

- Product traceability: food, cosmetic and medical use.
- Secure storage of information: Medical.
- Energy transfer automation: Smart contracts.

- Financial applications: Insurance and related services.

AT PRESENT, the Emurgo business team is made up of 6 managers attending to various areas occupied by a total of 43 employees. At the moment it shows a certain inclination to be focused on capturing and serving the English, Asian, Indian and Indonesian speaking markets.

The future of Cardano's development

If Cardano is an adequately staffed project today, it is never entirely a good thing for a blockchain to have centralized governance. The Voltaire phase of the project, the latest one, plans to completely decentralize governance to put Blockchain developments entirely in the hands of Cardano's shareholders, the holders of the ADA cryptocurrency.

Already repeatedly, through talks, conversations and interviews, Charles Hoskinson has talked about decentralizing governance. To this end, Cardano will be able to divide decision-making protocols into processes, and these processes in turn, will gradually be integrated into the blockchain. With more than 3,000 people currently involved in discussions about the structure of the blockchain and its future, there is no doubt that good ideas will emerge from within the community. As discussions progress, final proposals will emerge from the different communities and can be submitted for voting and consideration directly on the blockchain.

Blockchain will then be able to regulate through its shareholder group, when, how and to whom the money will be distributed for such purposes of the project. The project founders themselves will be directly responsible for providing all necessary data and information on the progress of the project to the community, and will be free to be closely monitored by certain members to facilitate access to further funding.

It seems obvious that IOHK, after having completed the 5 critical phases of the development of the Cardano Blockchain, will continue to be a player in it, because they will have earned the trust of the community and, let's put it this way; very well deserved. But this process will see the emergence of other companies, developers and ideas capable of evolving the blockchain and simultaneously working on their respective evolutions.

One aspect of great value peculiar to Cardano, a third-generation cryptocurrency and Blockchain that has been established and built on the basis of peer-reviewed studies, is the character that has led it to position itself and be considered the first scientific Blockchain in the cryptographic ecosystem.

If the crypto world has experienced growth and development in recent times; this has been directly proportional and in conjunction with Cardano; one of the most attractive projects existing in the third-generation crypto community. Cardano, a Blockchain whose basic and fundamental objective is to provide scalability, trust and security.

Cardano has dedicated great efforts and a high number of hours of work to achieve its clear and important objectives and technological advances, which are strictly interesting. This situation has allowed it to achieve goals and achieve important successes in its escalation of development in services and cryptographic character. At the same time, it has demonstrated that its Blockchain technology has a particular capacity to face all the challenges it encounters in the present to guarantee a more promising, enthusiastic and trouble-free future.

After two years of development, Cardano became a tangible reality. More precisely, on September 23, 2017, the first block of this cryptocurrency was successfully mined and began then, its immutable history. The name the project received is derived from the name of Girolamo Cardanos, a renowned and erudite Italian physician who became known for the first systematic probability calculations.

Cardano's native token became ADA, named after ADA Lovelace, a renowned woman with outstanding knowledge in mathematics, as well as being an English writer, well known for her work on the general-purpose mechanical computer, work proposed by Charles

Babbag, who was for that purpose; the analytical engine. From then on, the clear scientific note of the project is recognizable in all aspects.

In fact, Cardano stood out from the beginning with clear explanations, clear milestones and developments for the project. The idea behind this was not only to explain his work clearly, but also to show that the project was a clear and powerful long-term ambition. And that it was about solving problems such as scalability, looking for improvements in decentralization and in the security of the Blockchain technology itself.

This resulted in Cardano being classified as a third-generation blockchain. That is, with clearly established functions to send and receive values, to program smart contracts and to have an easily adaptable modular architecture.

Now, a little beyond all that we have exposed, it is worth saying that Cardano, has followed a clear path of development that has allowed it the possibility of reaching important milestones. And they have achieved this thanks to its valuable human capital involved and committed to the project, added to this, the presence of IOHK and the large scientific community of users and developers that has united around it.

Cardano's Roadmap, let's investigate in detail

Cardano is characterized for being a recognized Smart Contract platform conceived, planned and founded by Charles Hoskinson, who is also one of the co-founders that gave life to the emergence of the second largest cryptocurrency: Ethereum. However, Hoskinson was the driving hand that helped Ethereum to take off, the way he saw the way the plan would be put together was undoubtedly totally different from what was considered by those who were part of the working group. This situation and idea that was going around in his mind, caused Charles to decide at a certain point, to decline his responsibilities in front of Ethereum and put his position at the order; and thus, concentrate on the project that would give origin and life to the creation of its platform based on smart contract, an unpublished idea that resulted in Cardano.

The fact that makes Cardano a genuine protocol is that it is set up in several stages, each with its own importance and due importance at the same time. This is a very different approach than most other projects. Ethereum, for example, was launched all at once. The advantage of releasing all at once is that it allows the project to be adopted. Currently, Ethereum has the largest developer community and a big advantage in adoption over Cardano. The disadvantage is that by publishing everything at once, there will be bugs that can make the protocol susceptible to attacks.

By implementing the blockchain in stages, Cardano can release better code at the expense of sacrificing first-mover advantage. Which strategy is better? It's too early to say for sure. We'll have to wait and see what adoption of Cardano looks like once the project is fully developed.

Since its emergence over a decade ago, Blockchain networks have evolved significantly both in terms of technology and use cases. Heralded as one of the most innovative technologies of the new century, Blockchain aims to overhaul existing centralized systems across industries and eliminate their inefficiencies.

The first landmark event that marked the beginning of the Blockchain movement was, of course, Bitcoin. The world's first cryptocurrency runs on a first-generation blockchain based on the proof-of-work PoW consensus algorithm and was designed primarily to process transactions.

Ethereum arrived on the scene just a few years later, paving the way for today's burgeoning decentralized financial industry DeFi. The introduction of deployable smart contracts and decentralized application DApps was a game changer for the Blockchain industry, allowing it to scale to new heights and encouraging developers to experiment with new use cases for the technology.

When it comes to smart contract platforms, Ethereum currently dominates the space. However, issues such as network congestion, high transaction fees and network difficulties in scaling have held back the platform's potential over the years, which is why third-generation blockchains such as Cardano are increasingly gaining traction.

The Cardano protocol is still under development and its roadmap can be divided into five phases. Unlike most blockchain development teams, Cardano's approach is more modular. Although the phases are divided into different "eras", the Cardano team is working on all of them simultaneously. You can see that each era resembles a development track rather than a fixed timeline.

The First Phase

The Byron Era It took its name from Lord Byron, a poet and father of ADA Lovelace. This era marked the creation of the main architecture of the network. It also saw the implementation of basic protocol functionality to ensure the smooth operation of the network and its core technology.

Byron marks the initial launch of the Cardano (ADA) blockchain. A little-known fact is that Cardano's ticker symbol, ADA, refers to ADA Lovelace, who is often considered one of the world's first computer programmers.

Unveiled worldwide for the month of September 2017, Cardano was put on the market with a minimally variable product (MVP); by pate Byron as its head. Since then, those who use the network are able to carry out their sending and receiving operations, as well as safeguard their cryptocurrencies in Daedalus, the official wallet. In this way, all the power of Cardano would be palpable exclusively in new versions.

During this era, the Daedalus wallet, IOHK's official desktop wallet for ADA, was integrated into the Cardano ecosystem, as well as Yoroi, a lightweight wallet from IOHK's sister firm, Emurgo, which was designed for everyday use and offered efficient transaction and excellent performance.

The Second Phase: The Shelley Era

Established a greater degree of decentralization in the platform. Beginning with the launch of the Cardano core network, Shelley saw the Cardano ecosystem move away from the federated Byron era to a greater reliance on community-managed nodes. This era also saw the introduction of delegation and incentivization schemes.

Shelley was a big deal because he brought gambling to Cardano. The cryptocurrency community loves to gamble, and in the months leading up to Shelley's launch, Cardano's market cap increased significantly.

The Cardano team refers to Shelley as the decentralization milestone, as the introduction of Staking will decentralize validators. Simply put, in the first phase there were a small number of validators securing the Cardano network. Now that the second phase has been implemented, anyone can become a validator. This creates a more robust and secure network that is difficult to compromise.

Cardano aims to make betting as simple as possible for anyone to do so. Users can bet directly from the official Daedalus wallet or a third-party wallet such as Exodus. Betting on Cardano with Exodus is easy and straightforward.

The Third Phase: The Goguen Era

This third phase brought smart contracts to Cardano, enabling the creation of decentralized applications on the network using its smart contract development language, Plutus. During this time, Cardano also implemented a multi-currency ledger to facilitate the creation of new natively compatible tokens.

The Goguen upgrade will bring smart contract capabilities to the protocol. If there has been one consistent criticism of Cardano, it is that Cardano is a smart contract platform that doesn't have them. Even three years after its initial launch in 2017, it was still not possible to create smart contracts on Cardano. Currently, the scheduled launch date for Goguen, is on hold. It should be noted that this third phase was divided into three stages - Allegra, Mary and Alonzo.

The Allegra update was released on December 16, 2020 and the Mary update on March 1, 2021. The Alonzo update, which was further subdivided into three new phases: Blue, White and Purple, is still pending and awaited.

The total and expansive update of Alonzo was foreseen and planned to be launched in August 2021, this moment is still on standby, and the long-awaited presentation, sure to bring consolidation and greater value to Cardano, must wait a bit, as this new phase is still in the network section under important testing adjustments for its advancement.

Considering that Alonzo brings with it the long-awaited and long-awaited Smart Contracts functionality to the network, the community is eager to see it in action as soon as possible, as this already implies the enablement of decentralized applications (DApps) on its Blockchain.

One of the most interesting features that will make Goguen stand out will be its Marlowe programming language. The idea inside Marlowe is that it will allow its users, even without experience in software and programming issues to create smart contracts.

Another highlight of Goguen is that it will provide token support for Cardano. Developers will be able to generate and create their fungible and non-fungible tokens, the equivalent of the ERC20 and ERC721 token patterns in Ethereum.

The Fourth Phase: The Basho Era

It will involve scaling the Blockchain network, adding solutions focused on improving its performance and stability. It will also introduce interoperable sidechains, which will significantly help Cardano handle higher levels of performance, along with parallel accounting styles that can facilitate greater interoperability for Cardano and its applications.

The key feature of Basho is that it will bring sidechains to

Cardano. This will help the network scale so that it can handle significantly more transactions per second.

Sidechains are a way to perform transactions on a side network that is separate from the main Cardano base layer. The way a sidechain typically works is that transactions are performed in parallel. Periodically, all of these transactions will be batched and validated on the main chain. Because the transactions are performed on the sidechain, they are not affected by congestion on the main chain.

In terms of an analogy, a side-chain is like a road running alongside another expressway or freeway (the main chain). Cars can drive along the roadway (side-chain) and then, at periodic intervals, can access the freeway via an entrance ramp. There can be multiple sidechains along the Cardano Expressway and they can be customized to meet different design requirements.

The Fifth Phase: The Voltaire Era

This is designated as the final era of Cardano. Voltaire will establish an autonomous, decentralized network, transferring responsibility for the future of Cardano to the community. Instead of development and maintenance being carried out by a centralized entity such as the Cardano Foundation, the community itself will have the task of defending the network. The community will follow the example of Cardano's treasury, voting and proxy systems to accelerate its evolution into a decentralized, self-sufficient and complete protocol.

Participants will also be able to help the network grow by proposing enhancements for stakeholders to vote on, and the protocol will distribute transaction fees to fund various development activities suggested by these enhancement proposals.

This fifth, final phase will bring governance to the Cardano network. Like other networks, Cardano holders will be able to use their coins to vote on how Cardano's treasury should be spent and what kind of development work should be done in the network.

Cardano coin holders will be able to propose changes to the network, and then other users will be able to vote on those proposals.

Cardano expects this decentralized approach to maintaining and improving the network to be more beneficial than having a centralized organization making all the decisions.

Cardano is an ambitious project that aims to consolidate all the high-tech features of other blockchains in one place. Smart contracts, a proof-of-stake consensus mechanism, scaling across sidechains and a decentralized governance model. All of this requires a lot of work and more time than anyone would like, but the results should and promise to be the best expected for this valuable cryptographic scientific network.

Several teams and initiatives are currently building the Cardano ecosystem, but there are three key organizations that are currently primarily responsible for the development and maintenance of the blockchain. The core blockchain protocol has been created by the Switzerland-based independent non-profit Cardano Foundation, whose primary goal is to secure and promote the Cardano protocol and monitor ADA *tokenomics*.

The Cardano Foundation contracts with two other organizations to help build the network ecosystem, global Blockchain solutions platform, Emurgo and Blockchain research and development firm IOHK.

Emurgo is commonly referred to as Cardano's venture and commercial capital arm, while IOHK is Cardano's technology arm, which focuses on leveraging peer-to-peer innovations to provide financial services.

Cardano has attracted significant attention in recent times, especially with high gas rates and network congestion on Ethereum pushing DeFi applications to seek alternatives.

Cardano appears to be much stronger than Ethereum in terms of performance. Ethereum can handle 15 transactions per second (TPS) in its current state, although its proposed upgrade with *sharding* is expected to improve transaction speeds to nearly 100,000 TPS. By contrast, Cardano can already support hundreds of transactions per second, and with its Hydra layer 2 protocol under development, network throughput could increase to more than 1 million transactions per second.

In terms of smart contract capabilities, Ethereum is relatively less error tolerant, while Cardano's CCL offers more flexibility in case changes to deployed applications are needed. In addition, Cardano also allows users to set custom rules for confirming transactions.

However, Ethereum is poised to complete its migration from PoW to PoS and this modification could quickly shift the gyrations in its favor. The proposed release of Ethereum 2.0 Phase I in late 2021 should address many of the network's significant deficits. With networks like Cardano making Blockchain interoperability a reality, the industry may well gain more in the long run through collaboration, rather than competition.

Cardano vows for the possibility of establishing an ever greener Blockchain footprint, much lower, cheaper and higher yielding gas rates, which makes you believe the whole community to make it a preponderant space for NFTs, as well as the admission of mainstream DeFi, which are the two blueprints that each and every institutional investor is definitely very interested in.

Cardano vs Ethereum 2.0

Before we go into details about what differentiates one crypto from another and what details or aspects are against them, let's look at a concept concerning Cardano and Ethereum.

LET'S AGAIN DEEPEN, what is Cardano?

It is concrete, let's be clear and simple that Cardano is a Blockchain platform. It belongs to the third-generation proof of stake. What distinguishes it from other Blockchain platforms is its commitment to peer-reviewed scientific research on the process of updating the building blocks on its platform. The cryptocurrency used in transactions on this platform is "ADA". It was the co-founder of Ethereum who started developing Cardano in 2015 and finally launched it with great success in 2017.

The organizations responsible for the development and management of Cardano are IOHK, Cardano Foundation and Emurgo. Among these organizations, IOHK is responsible for the development of Cardano.

The above organizations are composed of two non-profit organizations which are IOHK and Cardano, while Emurgo, which is a for-profit company. The IOHK - Input Output Hong Kong includes a multidisciplinary team of scientists spread around the world to manage research and review platform updates prior to implementation so that changes are scalable.

Cardano is also a smart contract platform and has proven to Ethereum, which is itself, a great crypto alternative. Atala Prisma, Atala SCAN and Atala Trace are the products issued by the Cardano organization that maintains the Cardano services and image.

LET'S review again what Ethereum is?

Like its crypto partner, Ethereum is also a decentralized open source blockchain platform. It is the most active Blockchain platform on the network. Ethereum is the second largest marketplace after Bitcoin by market capitalization. Ethereum owns and uses "Ether" as the cryptocurrency for all transactions on the platform.

The programmer Vitalik Buterin proposed the concept of Ethereum in 2013, and then crowdfunding was organized in 2014. All these events led to the success of Ethereum when it went live on July 30, 2015 with the first shipment of 72 million coins.

It provides users with the service to start and run decentralized applications on the server. Another upgrade version is in the works that includes several improved facilities. The new version is called Ethereum 2.0 and includes the proof-of-stake transition, and its other goal is to increase transition performance by using *sharding*.

It is still a work in progress and will be released very soon. It is also open source and has smart contract functionality. The reason for being open source was Vitalik Buterin's vision to see it as a global "computer". Everyone has access to this "computer" so that anyone can start and run the application of their choice.

Basic differences between Cardano and Ethereum.

Revolution and self-improvement are the keys to human satisfaction. All efforts constantly to improve the day before, with the goal of achieving and attaining satisfaction. These continuous changes and improvements in mass efforts lead to revolutions that may take generations to recognize. One such new revolution is on its way that seems to be the future of the next generation: blockchain.

The process is still ongoing and in full development. Blockchain is a network that remains in frank and conscious growth, in total connection with cryptography, and its splicing units called blocks. Cardano and Ethereum are both crypto system platforms based precisely on the Blockchain, which offer the possibility of decentralized applications and intelligent contacts.

They are interesting operating systems on the network, which have been planned, designed and developed by duly conformed work teams that explore all areas of the crypto ecosystem to ensure the reliability, guarantee and security of a service that will henceforth "manage" economic resources and goods in a decentralized manner in complete tranquility; subject to the variants and fluctuations resulting from the same dynamics that automatically generates a changing global market system. Cardano, Ethereum and many other cryptocurrencies, seek as a basic objective; to satisfy their users around a myriad of their own requirements to their demands; that is when the race to success begins with a good proposal, sustainable, durable, stable and guarantor of equanimity in favor of those who decide to become part of the community in question.

Cardano vs Ethereum

The difference between Cardano and Ethereum is the native cryptocurrency used for all transactions on the platform. The native cryptocurrency used by Cardano for all transactions on the platform is the one known by the name ADA, while the native cryptocurrency within the Ethereum platform is Ether for all transactions.

Cardano is the first of the third Blockchain revolutions. It has two integrated layers. These two layers give the freedom to provide more rule sets in smart contracts. It is a proof-of-stake Blockchain platform. Cardano's development organizations are IOHK, Cardano Foundation and Emurgo.

Ethereum is a decentralized Blockchain platform. It is open source and has smart contract functionality. The native cryptocurrency on the platform for transactions is Ether. In all available blockchains, this is the most widely used blockchain. In terms of market capitalization, it has the second largest market worldwide after Bitcoin.

Main differences between Cardano and Ethereum

- Cardano is overseen by IOHK, Cardano Foundation and Emurgo, those organizations where IOHK is responsible for developing Cardano; while Ethereum is an open source platform.
- Cardano started development in 2015 and was launched in 2017, while Ethereum went live directly on July 30, 2015.
- The development of Cardano was carried out by Ethereum co-founder Charles Hoskinson, while the idea of Ethereum was proposed by Vitalik Buterin and funded by crowdfunding for development in the year 2014.
- Cardano uses ADA as the currency for exchanges, while Ethereum uses Ether for transactions.
- Organizations still maintain Cardano, while Ethereum is open source and available to all.

THROUGH A SIMPLE CHART, let's see a comparison between Cardano and Ethereum, these two important and even closely related cryptocurrencies, due to the fact of having in their beginnings and foundation; with the outstanding participation of Charles Hoskinson.

Comparative Parameters: Cardano vs Ethereum

Organization:

IOHK, Cardano Foundation and Emurgo are the organizations behind the development of Cardano.

It is a decentralized open source Blockchain platform.

ESTABLISHMENT:

The development started in 2015 and was launched in 2017.

It started its operations on July 30, 2015.

FOUNDATION:

It was developed by the co-founder of Ethereum, Charles Hoskinson.

It was proposed by Vitalik Buterin and the development was funded through crowdfunding in the year 2014.

PROPRIETARY (NATIONAL) CURRENCY:

Cardano uses ADA as the native cryptocurrency for its transactions.

Ethereum uses Ether as the cryptocurrency for transactions on the platform.

MAINTENANCE:

Cardano is managed by independent organizations.

Ethereum is an open-source platform where anyone can start and run an application.

THROUGHOUT THIS GALLOPING story within the transformative cryptographic digital race, virtual currencies are reaching their peak of greatest expression and the blockchain, in turn; is exploring its most accentuated benefits after a new technique to take advantage of it in a capital way and to the fullest.

Many blockchains are already in their rightful place, and these two:

Cardano and Ethereum, are just a sample of it. The fundamentals, bases and structures of the Blockchain remain the same, but the ideas, applications and techniques change with each of them, just like a guitar; with respect for comparison. The instrument is there intact and ready to be heard, it will sound, vibrate and captivate according to the way it is played by the musician who gives free rein to his skill, imagination and technique.

Many currencies through their respective Blockchain or structure, offer us additional services that will pretend to take them to the top and others are dedicated to participate in a competition to establish new and cutting-edge technologies in which others have not even come to imagine. Just like these cases, Cardano and Ethereum have their very marked and pointed some advantages over each other, so both are there, in the race, each competing to get each their deserved rung and recognized place within the crypto field and ecosystem.

While Cardano and Ethereum are preparing day by day to generate and offer important updates to the market, the most usual question we usually hear and read from most cryptocurrency investors is which of the two cryptocurrencies will generate a higher profit margin?

Last year 2020, both Ether and ADA managed to outperform Bitcoin. In the case of Ethereum, its rate has recently registered a considerable increase, going from 132USD to 241USD in mid-July 2021, which is equal to 82.5%, while Cardano's rate for its part has also manifested growth after a staggering 290%, climbing from 0.0330USD to reach 0.1285USD. All this against a remarkable contrast in view of modest growth for Bitcoin, of only 28%, remaining at the top of the virtual currencies.

The most interesting and manifestly relevant fact is that most of the growth experienced by Cardano occurred in a short period of time during the months of May and June. At the same time, Ethereum has also been growing steadily, even since the epic collapse of the crypto market recorded on March 12-13.

Both coins owe their remarkable performance in part to the general recovery in the crypto industry. However, we cannot leave aside another important and relevant influential factor in favor of this consequence, and that is the outstanding system of technical updates to which both Cardano and Ethereum are subject, this making reference to the particular case that concerns us in this chapter.

The long-awaited Ethereum 2.0 update has been delayed once again, possibly seeing the light of day until next January 2022. Meanwhile, for its part, Cardano is seen serene and calmly treading a very good path with its Shelley fork of last July 29.

It is the optimal management and utilization of the timing and content of these updates that best exposes, explains and determines the most salient dynamic price and value differences that represent and position Cardano and Ethereum within the network in favor of service for the crypto community and its distinguished users and customers.

CARDANO FT Ethereum

THE FOUNDING of Cardano occurred after Bitcoin and Ethereum was able to learn a great deal from those mistakes that BTC made, in order to leverage and learn from its own strengths. Founder and CEO Charles Hoskinson calls Cardano a third-generation cryptocurrency, meaning that ADA already has some of the same features that previous cryptocurrencies struggled to implement.

Cardano uses a modification of the proof-of-stake consensus algorithm called Ouroboros, which makes the network extremely scalable. At the same time, Ethereum is only planning to transition from proof-of-work to faster and more energy-efficient proof-of-stake. In this regard and without any discussion, ADA is already far ahead of Ethereum.

Another factor that plays a role in how Ethereum competes or differs from Cardano is the cohesiveness of its team. ADA is a commercial project and all programmers and researchers on the team are paid. Ethereum's developer community is a mix of mostly unpaid teams that argue with each other and present competing ideas constantly.

The fees on the ADA network are generally lower than on the Ethereum blockchain, while the transaction confirmation time is about the same. Basically, the only real, palpable advantage Ethereum has over ADA is the first-mover factor:

Ethereum is much more popular, a privilege it has well earned because of its pre-Cardano appearance, which is why it is much better known to the community, which is more accustomed to ETH. Some enthusiasts even refer to and label Cardano as the "Ethereum killer", although likely and most likely it is somewhat exaggerated.

Cardano keeps on going There are several factors that influence the steady rise that ADA continues to record after keeping on a steady march. Let's look at three of them, considered to be of great value, level and importance.

SHELLEY UPDATE: July 29, 2020.

This hard fork makes ADA much more decentralized and autonomous than Ethereum, but also more scalable and energy efficient. In particular, users will be able to delegate their shares in ADA and form participation groups. Currently there are already more than 200 groups in the test network. In addition, there is a clear direction for the next two upgrades. The first is Gougen, which will allow smart contracts to be aggregated and in turn build decentralized applications on Cardano; the second is Basho, which will introduce sidechains for even greater scalability. This news reinforces the already very optimistic mood.

STRONG RESISTANCE TO THE FIELD:

According to IntoTheBlock, most of the addresses held by ADA are now in the money, meaning they were purchased well below the current rate. This is what is shown in diagrams, schematics and graphs that can well be appreciated across the web. Through these resources the movements of interest in the crypto spectrum can be appreciated. A general dynamic is highlighted by the fact that those who have the money are not going to sell until they wait for the price to rise further, this creates what we call: Price Resistance.

DEVELOPMENT PARTNERSHIPS:

There is a new partnership with the Ergo blockchain protocol: This will allow Cardano to research stable coins and even offer decentralized financial services. decentralized. Another milestone is joining the Hyperledger consortium, which includes more than 250 Blockchain and financial companies.

As mentioned above, the main focus of the Ethereum community is the transfer to PoS, which allows users to receive rewards for staking their coins and validating transactions, as opposed to mining. More than 50% of Ethereum owners say they want to participate, so the long-term popularity of Ethereum PoS seems assured.

The upgrade, which will be introduced with PoS, was originally scheduled for July 2020, but as is common with Ethereum, it has been postponed. According to Vitalik Buterin, it should have happened at the time, but we will have to wait. However, Ethereum Foundation researcher Justin Drake says a date around January 3, 2022 is more realistic, which looms as possible.

Even if the 2021 update were to be released, it won't be a panacea for Ethereum's problems. It's just the first step on the road to full Ethereum 2.0, a way to test the new staking system without any critical applications relying on it.

No one knows how long to wait for a full transfer to PoS on the Ethereum main net. If things continue as they are, with endless debates and delays, we will have to be patient for at least half a year more.

Technical analysts are very bullish on Cardano at this current time. Nik "Altcoin Trader" Patel, for example, believes that the price can go up by as much as 55%, which represents an interesting value. Research firm Weiss Crypto Ratings is of the same opinion: "ADA is currently one of the most bullish-looking price charts of any major crypto asset. New highs were reached in 2020 and this one has proven to be able to continue that way."

Judging by the frequent updates released by the team, Cardano will stick to its plan and release updates as scheduled, so there should be no nasty surprises in terms of basic concepts. This will be an important factor in the race we see between Cardano and Ethereum.

As for Ethereum's course, the prevailing sentiment is that of a cautious optimist. At the time of writing, its price is 3,218.20USD, going steeply upwards, with a possibility of reaching 3,250.00USD. However, Ethereum still mainly follows Bitcoin's price movement, which is not very exciting at the moment. The recent postponement of the phase 0 update adds to the uncertainty.

Given these exposures, data and references, even uncertainties; it is up to the consumer or end customer to decide which coin to purchase. He will determine whether it will be Cardano or Ethereum. Overall, ADA seems to be more in favor of buying at this time, at least for short to medium term investors. At this point in time, late August 2021, Cardano sits at 2,774.34USD, gradually rising after a slight dip when it was quite close to 3,000.00USD.

However, the real decision will not be made until December or January, when Ethereum finally launches its phase 0 upgrade and will finally see how its PoS system prevails against Cardano's, who prepares its moment of success after the future activation of its phase 3 and the development of Smart Contracts.

The first places in the cryptographic ranking are very well identified and possessed by the biggest players in the market. Bitcoin as number 1 and Ethereum as the big number 2. They there are undisputed holders of a place that looks close to being replaced, but behind them, comes looking serene and patient within the crypto assets market; a coin that apparently would be mercilessly coming in second place. And yes, we are talking about Cardano ADA; which has been changing many analyses within the sector and has been visualizing very well the target or the center point of the negotiation.

AS THESE LINES ARE WRITTEN, the numerical face of these three coins is as follows:

- First Position: Bitcoin - BTC 48,739.67USD.
- Second Position: Ethereum - ETH 3,215.60USD
- Third Position: Cardano - ADA 2,76.60USD

THE MESSAGE IS CLEAR ENOUGH: the time of decision making for Bitcoin is over, now those blockchains that want to do better than Ethereum are getting ahead of themselves. After Polkadot made its way into the top 10 with the DOT token in recent months, the time has come then, for Cardano; which, through ADA in particular, is capturing and attracting the attention of the community.

But what makes Cardano special, besides the fast trading with the ADA token? The blockchain project was built around Charles Hoskinson, who originally worked for Ethereum. He has the company Input Output Hong Kong IOHK, which works together with the Cardano Foundation and Emurgo of Japan on the fundamentals and business models of Cardano. The big difference with

Ethereum remains that Cardano runs on the internal consensus algorithm Ouroboros on Proof of Stake (PoS) and is therefore where ETH 2.0 wants to go.

One notable difference of Cardano versus Ethereum and Bitcoin

More environmentally friendly Proof of Stake, at least that's how Cardano markets it, offers numerous advantages. Compared to Bitcoin or Ethereum, the Cardano blockchain should only need a fraction of the energy that Proof of Work (mining) would require. Y The possible transactions per second are much higher than with Ethereum, and as a PoS network, it is easier to incentivize users to participate in the network.

Proof-of-participation addresses the performance and energy usage challenges of proof-of-work and arrives at a more sustainable solution. It is important to note that for the Cardano case, the proof-of-participation makes an effective choice of participants in action groups to give rise to new blocks, with a foundation or root in their control in the network. This is in contrast to having to be in the hands of the well-known miners, in charge of solving complex computerized equations.

This allows networks to scale horizontally, increasing performance by adding additional nodes, rather than vertically, by adding more powerful hardware. The resulting difference in energy usage can be likened to that between a household and a small country. PoS is positioned at scale for the mass market; PoW is not.

All this is nothing new to Cardano insiders; in this 2021, years of preparations for many new applications will now appear to be paying off. Of course, the second Bitcoin hype also sweeps ADA, but there is also a foundation that makes it and the associated blockchain token attractive unlike other projects.

New opportunities for the community

Hoskinson's IOHK has handed over complete control of block production to the community, using the proof-of-stake algorithm to write the blocks on the chain themselves and be rewarded on return. In addition, an update should soon allow users to create their own tokens, which then function like ADA and the Cardano blockchain. These are the basic concepts to attract many more new users to Cardano, the crypto-scientist.

Many of these new users could come from Africa. In an interview, Hoskinson indicated that a government could be won as a customer on the African continent. With Atala PRISM, which is certainly not the optimal product name, Hoskinson's company, IOHK, has a Cardano application to implement digital identities. In the context of public authorities, it is conceivable that Blockchain could conceivably be used to make digital IDs unique and unalterable.

Another possible use case is represented by central bank digital currencies (CBDC). Elliot Hill of the Cardano Foundation brought the project into play through an article on central bank digital currencies. If states or power blocs like China or the EU are working on CBDC, it is feasible and manageable option to make the Cardano blockchain also become a technical basis for projects of other magnitudes of national interest.

Cardano is already and is in line with the trend, increasingly positioned in the area of *"Decentralized Finance"* (DeFi). Through smart contracts, an upgrade enables decentralized financial applications, for example in the area of lending. In the DeFi area, much smaller projects such as Chainlink, Aave or Uniswap have made a name for themselves, but Cardano's management also sees a lot of potential here and will not leave the field to others without fighting or working for it.

Frederik Gregaard, CEO of the Cardano Foundation, got involved in the debate about redesigning the financial system after the Game-Stop-Reddit-Robinhood story and, as expected; he advocated distributed accounting technologies. In addressing the financial sector, Frederik states that it is only now becoming known that the real problem that forced Robinhood to set higher margin requirements on certain positions was the intensity of trading activity. This was a situation that overloaded the capacity of multiple players in through its buying, selling and settlement process. In turn, this resulted in a backlog of settlement requests and subsequent liquidity issues for clearing houses.

With an open source blockchain infrastructure such as Cardano, any user is free to explore the code and develop solutions to implement on the project's blockchain. This is just one potential use case where the Cardano Foundation believes it can help innovate, and welcome change agents to its ecosystem who wish to push it forward.

In the face of this interesting development of processes, changes and updates that occur and present themselves as daily dynamics in the digital environment, and while many other projects in the cryptocurrency market in general has taken some respite, Cardano's ADA extended an impressive upswing, increasing its value and padding its trading volume on the token, becoming and remaining to date the third largest and most important cryptocurrency in the world, increased that has come amid anticipation of an upcoming software update that could help the token quietly compete with Ethereum.

Cardano's ADA continues to make leaps and bounds growing by significant percentages of up to 14% in just a matter of minutes, moving to a price of $2.74 USD from a point of $2.73 USD, according to crypto data website CoinMarketCap, raising its market capitalization above $88 billion USD.

Reflecting the fervor of its investors, billions of U.S. dollars worth of ADA tokens are generally exchanged on Thursdays in less than 24 hours, a high enough showing for same-day transactions. The token has been on a steady rise this month, climbing considerably since 2020, when Cardano founder Charles Hoskinson himself teased a September network upgrade, called Alonzo, that will enable the Cardano blockchain to process smart contracts, self-executing agreements between buyers and sellers a move capable of giving Ethereum the power to bring control in the face of growing $100 billion in decentralized merchant production free of government and financial dependencies.

Ethereum has been propelled to high levels in just three months over the past few weeks, all in the face of expectations for software updates and modifications. However, Cardano's latest network, in continuation of shelter and protection, has been allowed to catch the attention of suspicious characters, such as billionaire Mike Novogratz, a former hedge fund manager.

Novogratz, a die-hard Bitcoin fan and supporter, after watching ADA become the world's third largest cryptocurrency, expressed through his official Twitter handle that the token's rise represented a mystery to him, suggesting that his Platform faced a major struggle to reach a desired ground among software developers, creators of the precise programs for the takeover of a new digital currency.

Hoskinson, who also co-founded Ethereum, hit back at Novogratz, responding to a tweet touting that Cardano requires less energy than Ethereum to process transactions and mocking Novogratz's background in the traditional banking spectrum.

KEY BACKGROUND

CARDANO'S ADA token reached interesting highs last May, after the renowned and prominent billionaire Elon Musk, took an adverse attitude towards Bitcoin, stating that he would not receive Bitcoin again, due to the strong negative environmental impact generated by the mining of this cryptocurrency; because of its immense amounts of electricity consumption used in the process of obtaining new coins. The cryptographic system suffered a collapse from which it still awaits recovery, the opposite case for ADA; which had the opportunity to rise to higher levels of value as more and more investors were present in the massive acquisition of tokens more in tune with the natural environment. Charles Hoskinson, takes for granted, guaranteed and proven that Cardano only consumes an average of only 6 gigawatts of energy per hour of annual energy, not even 0.01% of the 115.85 Tera watts that per hour are used in the Bitcoin process.

The token plummeted nearly 60% as the broader market collapsed this summer, but has since begun to outperform Bitcoin and Ether.

There is one surprising fact, and that is the case that ADA has soared 1,300% this year alone, making it the best performing of the top five cryptocurrencies compared to returns of 1,030% for Binance Coin, 330% for Ether and 59% for Bitcoin. However, the token is also highly susceptible to massive volatility in the broader crypto market. At the start of 2018 and in just under eight weeks, ADA suffered a shocking drop of nearly 90%, for a time when regulations cracking down on the crypto market witnessed a scenario with market star-tups trending down for years, for nascent crypto manufacturing.

In the midst of Cardano's overnight rally, the overall cryptocurrency market rose less than 4% and floated around a total value of $2 trillion. The market soared above $2.5 trillion in May, but plunged amid concerns about regulations banning cryptocurrency mining in China.

When we talk about differences, we are not only referring to what each coin itself has, or what top or critical value it has reached or even experienced in its existence. We also seek to find those characteristics inherent in each token that in some way or another result in a benefit for the user, miner, developer, consumer and ecosystem in general.

That is to say, in which aspects who uses the network and consumes the coin, sees his life improved with the performance of a globally beneficial activity. In this even reaches certain subjective aspects of the individual, who like Elon Musk; see with concern the high levels of energy consumption that are necessary for the execution and activation of mining, basically with Bitcoin.

Influential people such as Musk, have been able to shoot the value of a cryptocurrency for its high degree of global satisfaction and incursion into its market of negotiations, but also, and depending on how it is constituted and structured its operational framework, it can declare that it declines in its use and consumption due to environmental affectations or dissatisfactions that have an impact on an unhealthy development for life, which in the end requires our best attitudes and creativity to build a world full of very good opportunities for all equally.

Conclude from your point of view, what would be the real differences you really consider relevant between these two great virtual currencies: Cardano ADA and Ethereum.

3

INVESTING IN CARDANO (ADA) TO MAXIMIZE YOUR RETURNS

C ardano is a promising project with a good amount of risks relative to what most cryptocurrencies are concerned. As you already very well know, it is a cryptocurrency that quickly gained traction after its launch on September 27, 2017.

Since then, the token has generated an impressive 7,080% to investors, far outperforming Bitcoin's range, which increased by 910% during the same period. As a result, Cardano is among the top 10 most valuable cryptocurrencies and today in third position, with a fully diluted market value of approximately USD 88 billion.

But the token is not without controversy. In fact, the idea behind Cardano has polarized members of the cryptocurrency community.

Cardano's ADA tokens are named after Augusta *"ADA"* King, a 19th century British countess known for her work on a theoretical computing engine. She is widely regarded as the first computer programmer.

The token was launched under the supervision of Charles Hoskinson, co-founder of Ethereum. Hoskinson parted ways with fellow co-founder Vitalik Buterin after the latter wanted Ethereum to remain a non-profit project. Hoskinson, however, wanted to take on venture projects to promote Ethereum. Thus, Cardano was born and continues to be developed by the for-profit Cardano Foundation.

Cardano is the first cryptocurrency based on a proof-of-stake (PoS) rather than proof-of-work (PoW) network. In PoW networks like Bitcoin, miners are responsible for validating transactions on the public Blockchain ledger by solving complex algorithmic puzzles via graphics processing units (GPUs). However, the difficulty of mining increases exponentially over time, so miners need to buy more advanced GPUs as time goes on, consuming more electricity. Anyone with multi-core central processing units (CPUs) could mine Bitcoin at the rate of about 50 or so per block in the early days, which is worth about 2 million USD today. Now, however; it would need a processor that is 2.2 billion times more powerful to keep up with the difficulty of mining.

All of this has serious environmental implications. Currently, one Bitcoin transaction uses as much power as approximately 1.2 million Visa (NYSE:V) transactions. At this rate and by the end of the century, Bitcoin's power consumption could easily exceed all of the world's energy production in BTC mining alone.

This is not supposed to be a problem with Cardano's PoS system. In this setup, those who hold the token, known as stakeholders, validate transactions instead of miners. Large stakeholders can earn an "interest" of 6.59% per year by managing a stakeholder group.

Those with smaller stakes can also delegate their Cardano tokens to a stakeholder group, earning roughly the same gross return before a 3.91% commission. But considering there are 32.9 billion Cardano tokens outstanding out of a total of 45 billion. So, the inflation-adjusted yield is less than 2%.

Investors can earn passive income from participation and capital gains from price appreciation. At the same time, the network probably uses as much energy as a city of a few thousand people compared to Bitcoin, which consumes the equivalent of the entire power supply for a country with an average population of 20 million.

The token is becoming increasingly innovative. By 2020, the Cardano Foundation launched token sharding, which allows the partitioning of the network into local, stakeholder nodes. This enables faster processing times of 1,000 transactions per second per node or 1 million transactions per second for the entire network. By the end of the year, Hoskinson plans to integrate smart contract functionality, which will allow Cardano to match the utility of Ethereum.

One possible unstable reality is in the PoS network, which could create difficulties while solving them. The setup gives crypto whales, high net worth investors, a disproportionate amount of power on the blockchain. A whale cannot disrupt a PoW network unless it also controls 51% of the blockchain's computing power to perform a hash attack.

However, the same whale could easily launch an attack vector against a PoS network by simply controlling 51% of the outstanding supply. So far, Cardano has not succumbed to consolidation. More than 2,656 mining pools control 71% of its total supply.

The biggest problem Cardano faces is lack of adoption. At the moment, it is mainly start-ups using the technology, although it has some major partners such as Price waterhouse Coopers and Wolfram Alpha, an engine that solves complex mathematical problems, especially popular in academia. It has also failed to attract much attention from governments, apart from small countries like Georgia.

With its strong market capitalization, investors are clearly pricing in the possibility of a smart contract implementation leading to wider adoption of the network. Of course, that could be possible. But until that happens, I would rate Cardano as suitable for speculative investors only.

If you need to invest, you also need to know where and how you will invest. Cardano is a fully public, third-generation Blockchain and Dapp development platform. Cardano, as a cryptographic platform deserved to capture outstanding attention through various media and channels worldwide, being categorized as the first Blockchain to insert valuable investigative expertise by peer review in its basic initial foundations. Currently, ADA is recognized and established as one of the world's leading digital currencies, in third position after Ethereum.

It tends to be recurrent and quite regular that both renowned analysts and major investors refer to Cardano as a third-generation digital currency. Specifically, Bitcoin; as a first-generation currency, had the ability to insert into the network, globally; a system or method of decentralized money with security and confidence.

Third-generation cryptocurrencies, such as ADA, use new developments, such as layered architecture, to improve scalability, security and sustainability. In doing so, they create more utility, address flaws and rectify inefficiencies.

Why Cardano (ADA) is important?

Cardano is a very important cryptocurrency given its difference from the competition in many and varied aspects, of which we have seen the most relevant. In contrast to its counterparts, Cardano relies heavily on academia. The platform's design was built from the ground up using evidence-based methods based on scientific philosophy, academic theory and finalized through peer-reviewed research.

Remember, the name Cardano comes from the famous Italian scholar and physician, Girolamo Cardano. Cardano changed the world after developing the first systematic probability calculations. His legacy is still alive and well today.

A wide range of outstanding goals for the Cardano Project are in the hands of its developers. It is a valuable and very well trained team that has been dedicated to achieve the rescue of familiarity and confidence in the global mercantile and economic procedures, through the incorporation of Cardano's own technologies. Very specifically, this platform has the ability to provide a much more secure, reliable, credible and clear structure for the execution of procedures and negotiations at all geographic levels.

In addition to this, it is worth mentioning that Cardano's developers, dig deep to offer the entire crypto community, financial accessibility free of ties to government agencies, private, traditional banking or monitored by third parties. Current statistics are not at all encouraging, when they place the unbanked demographic mass at over 1.7 billion people today.

Based on the above, there is an economic project launched for the African region and several areas of the world, already in clear development, by Cardano.

An intention of relevance and great socio-economic and cultural impact.

Cardano's third objective is to help stabilize the Dapp sector. The platform focuses on security and sustainability with a specific focus on decentralized applications, systems and societies. Speaking about their goals, Cardano's developers stated that they intend to provide a more balanced and livable ecosystem that is more responsive to the needs of its users, as well as other systems seeking integration.

Being recognized and standing out as a third-generation digital currency, Cardano is making great efforts to face certain and certain conflicts, which otherwise tend to be quite recurrent, that force the incorporation of Blockchain at larger scales. These issues cover blockchain tactics, including issues such as scalability, interoperability and sustainability. These conflicting situations, tend to be controlled and subdued by Cardano, through its development programs with planning principles and strategies with satisfactory answers in its engineering.

. . .

SCALABILITY:

Just taking its first steps in the cryptographic ecosystem, Cardano had the limited capacity to process a maximum of 10 transactions per second (tps). However, Hoskinson released a statement, making it clear and explicit what the novel scaling procedure would mean for the network: Hydra.

Hydra is a Layer 2 scaling solution that uses stateful channels to process off-chain transactions. With this technology, Cardano can process more than one million transactions per second.

INTEROPERABILITY:

At the present time, and reviewing the network, we can see the coexistence of thousands of digital currencies available globally, each one with its own particular aspects and enough of its own, with great benefits and particular ecosystem. We see how, in the face of this growing demand, Cardano is doing everything in its power to incorporate into the market certain standards that facilitate interoperability between enabled and active networks. These systems include Blockchain governance models, system update protocols and feature sets.

SECURITY:

Enabling Blockchain interoperability introduces a new set of risks that developers must address. These security concerns are one area where Cardano plans to reign. Currently, the platform has standards in place to manage privacy, security and decentralization.

OUROBOROS:

Ouroboros is a consensus component that was launched and activated by Cardano as an important new feature. The formality that constitutes Ouroboros is of the PoS type, conceived in chain. It is based on randomly selected guides or ringleaders in order to certify blocks. In the same way as the vast majority of existing Blockchains, the node attached to the contiguous block is incentivized with an award or reward, as it is commonly known. All this for its merits to the efforts deployed.

At the beginning of each season or period, the system tends to choose team leaders from areas of importance. Seasons function as a snapshot of the blockchain from a previous date. It must have, fundamentally at its inception its own solidly structured blockchain and large bases in its transaction chain. It is imperative to have an appropriate sinkhole, which will be useful to validate the full security of the network and to be far from being a victim of invasive transformations in the chain.

The technicalities of this system are impressive. The tendency is to choose group leaders, according to the deployment of fixed action and a random seed. A procedure of multiple part calculations (MPC) is used for this seed, among the parts of interest, which form or conjugate the preceding epoch of random generation. Those who aspire to be selected have every chance to optimize their ability to be selected according to the number of ADAs put into play or bet. Consequently, Cardano presents the first demonstrably secure participation testing protocol.

HISTORY OF CARDANO (ADA)

CARDANO ENTERED the market in September 2017. Two prominent figures, who fulfilled the mission of founding the project were, Jeremy Wood and Charles Hoskinson, who came from rows in favor of Ethereum. Despite this, the staff decided to leave Ethereum, emphasizing relevant disagreements in the objectives.

Almost instantly, Cardano benefited from a positive pursuit within the cryptographic spectrum; thanks to its outstanding novelties in everything related to and inherent to language and outline of virtual devices. Everything that added up, was given in clear and direct response to difficulties found in the Ethereum network, against which there were serious discrepancies. The platform managed to differentiate itself from the competition and began to collaborate with professors from prestigious universities around the world to incorporate academic research into its design.

To raise funds, an ICO was conducted. The platform raised approximately 62 million USD from a global audience of investors. The funds were earmarked for the expansion of the ADA ecosystem.

On September 29, 2017, Cardano launched its first app on the main-net. This was how the beginning of a journey full of achievements for those who were already part of and constituted the team was established. Already by 2018, Cardano saw clearly guaranteed a great diversity of partnerships and multiple partnerships of the highest and most relevant level, such as in the academic and FinTech sectors.

By 2019, the Huobi organization already included ADA. While Huobi was consolidating its position as the largest exchange in the Asian giant, it had to relocate as a result of regulatory pressure. All this, shortly after having been part of the exchange with the greatest impact worldwide. Binance also incorporated ADA into its platform. These important situations gave ADA the most expected boost and growth in price, value and recognition. They elevated it to new and great heights within the network.

ADA tokens are named after the 19th century mathematician, ADA Lovelace. Lovelace was the world's first computer programmer. Currently, there are more than 32,143,026,588 ADA tokens in circulation. In total, Cardano will issue 45,000,000,000,000 ADAs during its lifetime.

CARDANO EQUIPMENT:

Cardano utilizes a decentralized team of developers. These developers work in three separate entities. Importantly, they use established standards to ensure interoperability within the ecosystem. Each team provides its own support to the project.

. . .

CARDANO FOUNDATION:

The Cardano Foundation is the non-profit entity behind the platform. This foundation protects the protocol technology and ensures its functionality. In addition, they promote standardization in the industry for greater interoperability.

INPUT OUTPUT HONG KONG - IOHK:

IOHK is a science and engineering company that develops technologies behind the network. They also design and maintain these protocols through a two-pronged approach. First, the group investigates the fundamentals of cryptocurrencies to uncover core concerns. These issues include theoretical discussions about which consensus algorithms and privacy protocols are best.

Then, the engineering side of the team begins the development process. To accomplish this task, the team uniquely incorporates formal methodologies. This strategy gives Cardano an additional layer of approval.

EMURGO:

The final piece of the ADA puzzle is Japanese incubator Emurgo. This team focuses on commercial enterprises and how to advance the use of Blockchain technology across industries.

GOVERNANCE:

The governance system used in Cardano is similar to Ethereum. The network has a decentralized autonomous organization (DAO) to approve new initiatives. DAOs are ideal for making decisions about the future of cryptocurrencies because they help prevent community divisions.

Cardano Controversy

Despite its heavy reliance on academics, there are still some in the industry who pointed out potential problems with the network. Specifically, Ethereum PoS researcher Vlad Zamfir argues that blockchain voting is dangerous. He points out that the system forces rule changes on entire nodes. This strategy removes an important check and balance provided by informed node operators.

Cardano - The Academic Blockchain

Given its huge and growing network of followers, it is safe to say that Cardano will remain a staple in the Blockchain industry for years to come. Its unique approach and technical advancements are sure to remain a hot topic within the industry as development progresses. For now, ADA remains among the top 15 cryptocurrencies in the world. And remember, it's the third most important coin.

WHERE TO BUY Cardano and which Wallets support this cryptocurrency?

ONCE YOU KNOW HOW, you may find that buying Cardano is a fast, secure and easy process.

Cardano is a popular choice among cryptocurrency investors looking for projects with strong long-term potential. By now Cardano is in a prime position in the crypto rankings, it is the third largest digital currency by market capitalization. Unlike market leaders Bitcoin and Ethereum, Cardano does not require a lot of energy, which makes it an environmentally friendly cryptocurrency.

Let's see what we need to address the right place and process to buy Cardano.

· · ·

FIND an exchange that sells Cardano

START by selecting a crypto exchange where you can buy Cardano. Because Cardano is one of the largest coins, many of the best cryptocurrency exchanges list it. Here are some of the most popular crypto exchanges and investment platforms through which you can buy Cardano:

- Coinbase
- Binance
- Kraken
- eToro
- SoFi
- Easy Crypto

THE TWO MAIN most important conditions you should look for in a crypto exchange are security and reasonable fees, offered by all these platforms.

For beginners, Coinbase is a great option due to its ease of use. It doesn't take long to learn how to trade cryptocurrencies using Coinbase, which also provides a lot of educational content to its users.

BINANCE:
The best choice for Australia, Canada, Singapore, UK and most of the world. US residents are banned from many of the tokens on this platform. You can get started and sign up here and get a discount on all your transactions:

KRAKEN:

This exchange is the best option for residents of the United States.

ETORO:

With its operating offices located Great Britain, Israel and Cyprus, this is a broker with dedication and specialization in Social Trading, through which you can operate diversity of instruments is a broker specializing in social trading, which operates multiple financial instruments, including: stocks, currencies and cryptocurrencies among others.

SOFI:

American exchange company, which operates as a mobile personal finance service, based in San Francisco. SoFi offers a diverse menu of financial products including student loan refinancing, mortgages, personal loans, credit cards, investments and banking through its mobile app and desktop interfaces.

. . .

EASY CRYPTO:

A fabulous regulated exchange is the best for Australia, New Zealand and South Africa.

SIGN up for an account

You need an account with your chosen exchange to buy cryptocurrencies. The registration process depends on the exchange, but on most you'll find a button that says "Get Started", "Register" or "Register".

Exchanges usually ask for the following information to open an account:

- Full names
- Email address
- Phone number

THE EXCHANGE MAY REQUIRE you to set up two-step authentication. With this feature, you must go through two layers of security when logging into your account. For example, instead of simply entering your password, you will also need to enter a code that the exchange sends to your email address or phone number.

Even if two-factor authentication is not required, it's worth setting it up on your account for added protection.

VERIFY YOUR IDENTITY (KYC)

ONCE YOU'VE CREATED your account, it's time to verify your identity. Cryptocurrency exchanges must do this with their customers to confirm their identities and prevent illegal activities, such as money laundering.

Again, the exact process depends on the exchange, for this you should be prepared to provide the following information:

- Date of your birthday.
- Social security number.
- Physical address.
- Scan of a valid ID, such as your driver's license or passport.

PLANNING your investment strategy to ensure returns (ROI) The best approach with cryptocurrencies is to treat them as a long-term investment. And if you are going to treat it as such, an investment; it is helpful to have a defined strategy. You can plan your cryptocurrency investment by answering the following questions, for example:

- How often will you buy Cardano? Some people make one big purchase and wait to see what happens. Others buy on a regular basis, such as every two weeks or every month.
- How much will you invest? This will depend on your risk tolerance and how often you plan to buy more. If you are going to buy Cardano frequently, you may not want to buy a large amount on your first try.
- When do you plan to sell your Cardano? You can go with a time period such as holding your Cardano for at least five years, a target price, or a combination of the two.

Here is an example of an investment strategy

My plan is to buy 250USD worth of Cardano every month. I will hold it for at least five years, but if the price triples before then, I will withdraw my original investment to make sure I don't lose money.

That's just one option, and your strategy can be as simple or complex as you wish. By having a plan in place, you don't need to wonder what to do every time the price of Cardano goes up and down.

MAKE your Cardano purchase

CHECK which payment methods the crypto exchange you have selected accepts and the fees for each. These are the most common payment methods you will encounter:

- Bank transfer
- Debit Card
- Credit Card
- PayPal

MOST MAJOR EXCHANGES allow you to deposit cash from a bank account at no charge. You still pay transaction fees when buying cryptocurrencies, but it ends up being cheaper than other payment methods. With debit cards, credit cards and PayPal, you pay more in fees on your cryptocurrency purchase. Just keep in mind that the transfer process from a bank account can take a few business days.

Once you have the funds in your exchange account, choose the amount of money you want to spend on Cardano. The exchange will show you a preview of the transaction with the fees and the amount of Cardano you will receive. If it looks right and you agree, confirm your new purchase.

After doing this, the Cardano you purchased should be available in your account in just a few seconds. The last thing you should consider is moving your Cardano to a crypto wallet. Since crypto wallets provide more security, they are a popular way for investors to protect their coins.

Buy and sell cryptocurrencies on an exchange chosen by experts You know, there are hundreds of platforms around the world that are waiting to give you access to thousands of cryptocurrencies. And to find the one that suits you best, you will have to decide which functions are the most important for you, and the ones that best meet your expectations.

How to store Cardano (ADA)

The three most popular ways to store your ADAs are in a desktop wallet, a mobile app, or a hardware wallet. Each of these strategies has its own characteristics. You may find that one doesn't fit all of your needs. In this case, use a combination of all three.

An excellent alternative for all those who recently enter the crypto environment, is represented in a mobile wallet. It is a resource that can be safely downloaded, it is free, easy to set up and very secure. For this reason, those who are starting to invest in cryptocurrencies should do so by taking this step. More experienced users will opt for a desktop client because of the security it provides.

Anyone looking to make a large investment in ADA should consider buying a hardware wallet. Hardware wallets are more secure than mobile wallets because they keep your cryptocurrency securely stored offline in cold storage.

THE LEDGER NANO S or the more advanced Ledger Nano X, are compatible with Cardano.

. . .

CARDANO IS an innovative Blockchain platform that provides robust security and sustainability for the development, systems and partnerships of decentralized applications (DApps). This platform with a multi-asset ledger and verifiable smart contracts helps run financial applications used by individuals and institutions worldwide.

ADA is Cardano's native token, which can be used as a secure exchange of value. Users can store their Cardano (ADA) in secure wallets to delegate to a participation group and earn rewards.

Below, we will show you more details in a carefully selected and interesting list of the best pro-Cardano wallets with popular features and links to websites. The list contains both free open source and paid commercial software.

BINANCE:

One of the best platforms for creating a Cardano wallet that offers a platform for trading more than 150 cryptocurrencies. It provides an API that helps you integrate your current trading application. You can get started and sign up here:

FEATURES:

- This application offers a wide range of online trading tools.
- It is one of the most secure Cardano wallets that provides 24/7 support.
- This platform is compatible with web, iOS, Android and PC clients.
- Binance offers basic and advanced exchange interfaces for trading.
- It has an average daily trading volume of 1.2 billion with over 1,400,000 transactions per second.
- Supported currencies: BTC, BCH, LTC, ETH and Cardano.
- Hardware wallet support: Ledger, Trezor only.
- Security: High
- Wallet type: Software

COINBASE

ONE OF THE best Cardano wallets that can be used to buy, sell, transfer and store digital currency. It securely stores a wide range of digital assets in offline storage. This platform supports more than 100 countries. You can buy Bitcoin and other Cryptocurrencies here:

Features:

- You can buy and sell any digital currency and keep track of them in one place.
- Provides an app for iOS and Android devices.
- You can schedule your forex trading on a daily, weekly or monthly basis.
- It stores your funds in a vault for security purposes.
- It is one of the largest cryptocurrency exchanges.
- You get 5USD in Bitcoin free for signing up.
- Supported currencies: BTC, BCH, LTC, ETH, Cardano and others.
- Hardware wallet compatibility: Only with Ledger, Trezor.
- Security: High
- Wallet type: Software

Gemini

. . .

ONE OF THE best Cardano wallets that helps you to legitimize cryptocurrencies worldwide. It is a simple, elegant and secure way to create a cryptocurrency wallet.

FEATURES:

- It offers discounts of up to 0% for volume traders.
- Offers good security measures.
- Supported currencies: Bitcoin, Ethereum, Litecoin, Cardano and Bitcoin Cash, etc.
- Hardware wallet support: No
- Security: Standard
- Wallet type: Software

Kraken

IT IS one of the best Cardano wallets that offers financial stability by maintaining full reserves, relationships and the highest standards of legal compliance.

FEATURES:

- Comprehensive security approach.
- Allows you to buy and sell assets with a single click.
- You can communicate with your support team via live chat.
- Kraken automatically checks all addresses for errors.

- Supported currencies: BTC, Litecoin, Cardano, Dash, Zcash, etc.
- Hardware wallet compatibility: Yes
- Security: High
- Wallet type: Software
- Supported platforms: Web, iOS and Android

Trezor

IT IS a hardware wallet that helps you store your Cardano coins. You can easily connect it to your computer or smartphone. it helps you to randomly generate a PIN code that keeps the device safe and secure.

YOU CAN BUY the latest **TREZOR MODEL T here:**

Or maybe you are interested in the **TREZOR MODEL ONE:**

FEATURES:

- Offers ultra-secure offline storage.
- Supports over 1,000 coins.
- Easy to use touch screen.
- Extremely simple to use.
- Allows you to hide your private key.
- Currencies supported: BTC, ETH, BCH, LTC, Cardano, XLM, HT, USDC, Dash, etc.
- Supported platforms: Windows, Mac OS X or Linux.
- Wallet type: Hardware
- Security: High

Coinsmart

IT IS a digital currency exchange that allows you to buy and sell cryptocurrencies seamlessly. It allows you to access your crypto balance instantly. This app gives you a quick and easy way to invoice your customers using SmartPay Invoicing.

FEATURES:

- Provides 24/7 live support.
- Allows you to trade any currency with a single click.
- Processes all Fiat withdrawals within a few days.
- Allows you to place customized orders seamlessly.
- This platform can be accessed from mobile devices and desktop computers.
- Supports cryptocurrencies: Bitcoin Cash, XRP, Litecoin, Cardano and more.

LEDGER NANO

THE LEDGER NANO is a hardware wallet that supports a multitude of cryptocurrencies. This hardware wallet has an LED display for payment validation and a PIN to confirm the transaction. This handheld device is convenient and secure.

CHECK THE LEDGER NANO S HERE:

Features:

- You can easily access it through USB compatible devices.
- It allows you to install up to 100 applications.
- This Cardano wallet allows you to protect and control all your cryptocurrencies.
- It offers 2-factor authentication.
- Supported platforms: Windows (7+), Mac (10.8+) and Linux.

CEX.IO

THIS IS one of the best Cardano wallets that helps you buy and sell cryptocurrencies. It allows you to deposit funds with MasterCard, Visa card or PayPal Debit MasterCard. This platform follows frequency trading and scalping strategies to protect assets and data.

VISIT **CEX.IO and see prices here:**

FEATURES:

- Users can trade USD for ADA, Bitcoins, Ethereum and XRP (Ripple).
- Protects against DDOS (distributed denial of service) attacks through full data encryption.
- It can trade with more than 10x leverage without creating an additional account.
- It is one of the leading encryption exchanges that supports platforms such as mobile devices and websites.
- This DApp offers downloadable reports showing real-time balance and transaction history.

Cardano Wallets

Cardano Wallet is a cryptocurrency wallet that allows you to send, receive, store and manage Cardano cryptocurrency (ADA). Cardano wallets are available on software, hardware, online and app platforms. It offers robust security for cryptocurrency transactions.

. . .

ADVANTAGES OF CARDANO:

- Here are some pros / benefits of Cardano:
- Ensures mathematical accuracy in Cardano's operation.
- Helps you reduce energy costs when verifying blocks.
- Allows you to make fast transactions to work with digital assets.
- Cardano does not charge large fees when performing instant transactions.
- Complete anonymity of users.
- Corrects network errors without a back hook.

CAN I store my cryptocurrencies in two or more wallets at the same time?

NO, you cannot store all cryptocurrencies in the same wallet and not all locations store the same cryptocurrencies. Some wallets can store only 3 cryptocurrencies, and they are divided into three different wallets and have the vault options. However, some wallets also allow storing more than 3 cryptocurrencies.

THE BEST CARDANO wallet for Android

SOME GOOD CARDANO wallets for Android are Coinbase, Gemini, Binance, Kraken, etc.

Best Cardano wallet for iOS Some good Cardano wallets for iOS are Coinbase, Gemini, Binance, Kraken, etc.

Tips for securely storing your Cardano

- Go offline: Offline storage eliminates the threat of hacking, making it more secure than any internet-connected wallet.
- Backup: Make sure to back up your wallet regularly so that it is up to date. You can easily access your encrypted holdings in case something goes wrong.
- Use common sense: You should use a strong password and never give out passwords or private keys to anyone else.
- Choose a reliable wallet: Make sure you always choose a reliable and reputable crypto wallet.
- Cardano wallets that can be used for staking.
- Ledger Nano X, Coinbase, etc., can be used for Cardano staking.

4

THE BEST DEFI PLATFORMS BUILT
ON CARDANO'S NETWORK

T he Cardano project was started in 2015 by Input-Output
Hong Kong - IOHK, an organization managed by Ethereum
co-founder Charles Hoskinson. The idea behind Cardano
was and is to create a blockchain that works much better than more
established blockchains like Ethereum and Bitcoin.

This means being able to process more transactions reliably at
lower costs and with lower energy consumption. Its primary use case
is for developers to create secure applications powered by Cardano
using its native ADA governance token. Cardano is a vast ecosystem,
a massive project with many components, both in the technical and
organizational sense. Its blockchain itself consists of the Cardano

settlement layer (CSL) and the Cardano computation layer (CCL). CSL is used to transfer ADA between accounts and CCL contains the smart contract logic used by applications to move funds programmatically.

Cardano features the Ouroboros protocol, represented by an ancient Egyptian symbol depicting a snake eating its own tail. It is also the name of the proof-of-stake (PoS) consensus algorithm used by nodes running Cardano software. Time is divided into epochs and slots, the former representing general time frames and the latter 20-second intervals. Within each slot, a random leader is chosen to add the next block to the blockchain, after which the coin is flipped again to choose the next slot leader.

Within Cardano, nodes represent the maintenance of the blockchain, which in due operation is done through a very well distributed network.

THREE TYPES of nodes apply to Cardano:

- Edge: To create transactions in cryptocurrencies.
- mCore: Bet on ADA and participate in distributed governance.
- Relay: Send data between mCore and the public Internet.

IN ITS ORGANIZATION, Cardano is maintained by a collection of separate organizations. The Cardano Foundation is based in Switzerland and is in charge of overseeing the development of the Cardano blockchain. Emurgo is the business development unit that socializes the product in the institutional space. IOHK built Cardano and Ouroboros.

Cardano development takes a different approach Cardano has many familiar features, such as running smart contracts to create decentralized applications (dApps). What makes it different is its research-based approach to building the foundations. Optimizations are based on scientific research and formal peer-reviewed verification. For example, Ouroboros has been deemed demonstrably secure through formal review.

The purpose is to create a robust protocol that meets business standards. In support of that goal, Cardano's code is written in the Haskell programming language, which is used in the banking and defense sectors.

At the time of writing, IOHK has published just over 100 scholarly articles in its library covering technology and fostering partnerships with universities around the world, with the firm intention and best intentions of facilitating learning and building knowledge that best illustrates the need-to-know and need-to-know about Cardano.

Creation of a token: ADA

Named after the 19th century mathematician ADA Lovelace, ADA is the native token used for transactions and participation in governance on the Cardano blockchain. You must own ADA to become the next slot leader following the PoS model, vote on software policies such as inflation rates, and determine who earns a share of fees paid for blockchain transactions.

The token was launched during Cardano's ICO in 2016 with a total of 62 million USD. After it became available for trading on the crypto markets in 2017, the price rose 6,050% from 0.02USD to 1.23USD in just 3 months. Those were the frenzied days of the ICO when the moon seemed closer than ever. Since then, the price has been correcting from 0.07USD and 0.04USD for most of 2018 to the present. ADA has been steadily rising. As of today, the token is trading at 2.58USD.

Cardano's rise is impressive. What's behind it?

First, the implementation of the Shelley upgrade has created more interest in the protocol, as its participation system offers rewards, incentive schemes and low fees. These are attractive features for investors in the Cardano protocol. Second, CEO Charles Hoskinson has started making a play for DeFi by saying in a video that Cardano could win the race for decentralized finance. The DeFi game is heating up and any project that puts itself in a position to play a leadership role will reap the rewards in both adoption rates and token valuation.

If Cardano really is up to the task of winning the race for DeFi, ADA presents a great growth opportunity for both the organization itself and for traders in crypto markets looking to profit from DeFi's rapid expansion.

The initial DeFi project for Cardano has changed from Polkadot, a transformative Blockchain plan that focuses on creating a much more secure interactive infrastructure between the various existing blockchains, all while bringing scalability alternatives and new functionality.

The Bondly platform will process the transition of its digital currency, OTC BSwap and e-commerce platform BONDProtect to Cardano from Polkadot.

Bondly is a decentralized electronic trading platform, which will become the first financial project to be executed as part of running Goguen's functional smart contract platform on the Cardano Blockchain.

In an announcement via social network Twitter, the company that created the Cardano platform made mention of IOHK, referring to it as the partnership that has taken a big step in advancing the two companies' mission in bringing decentralized finance to the masses.

The start of Goguen, which was due to be completed in February 2021, enables the development of decentralized applications on the network and marks the beginning of the integration of DeFi projects into the Cardano ecosystem. IOHK CEO Charles Hoskinson said the deployment of applications such as Bondly on the platform would enable DeFi to reach its true potential and eventually completely replace the digital financial system globally.

Just as the upgrade continues on its path, Bondly will move its BONDLY cryptocurrency from Polkadot to Cardano, as will the company's two flagship products. The well-known over-the-counter BSwap trading platform and BONDProtect, a well-known e-commerce platform, offer a decentralized repository and buyer protection.

In contrast to Ethereum, where ETH trades are more significant than those executed with ERC-20 tokens, the Goguen upgrade will not override Cardano's trading activities over other tokens issued on the platform. This provides a better benefit for non-local tokens that will benefit from all the security features and ADA smart contracts of the original Cardano token.

After the full implementation of Cardano's Goguen upgrade, the platform's Marlowe project will commence. The initiative will allow peer-to-peer advances and contracts for difference (CFD) directly with Cardano. Platform users can publish ready-to-use templates for their DeFi contracts and digital assets, and then transfer the contract terms to the platform.

As of mid-December 2020, the company notified about another new DeFi project called Liqwid, as a very good potential contender for 250,000USD ADA under Project Catalyst.

Hoskinson has always been known for having very high ambitions and expectations for Cardano. During the first half of 2020, he suggested that Cardano be transformed into a leader in the DeFi sector. Earlier in the same year, the IOHK CEO predicted via a live broadcast on January 3, 2020, on his YouTube channel that Cardano would replace Bitcoin as the number one cryptocurrency by the end of the year. That's something that hasn't happened yet. For the time being we remain vigilant as to what such a prediction might generate.

Wave Financial Group recently partnered with Cardano to produce an in-depth report, "Cardano: From Ideation to Manifestation," with perspectives and insights on key trends in blockchain and crypto. The report covers the DeFi landscape and the "three tabs" of blockchain: scalability, interoperability and sustainability, as well as Cardano's solution through Wave's unique cFund. This is an early-stage crypto-native hedge fund that is taking a venture capital approach to drive Cardano's expansion.

Global financial inclusion is a fact. The development of Cardano was initiated by Input Output Global (IOG) with the mission of achieving global financial inclusion. IOG's goal in building and testing the blockchain was to ensure the scalability, interoperability and sustainability of the network. Certainly a lofty goal, but if achieved, the network can be transformed into a powerful new economic infrastructure that will provide unprecedented access to critical financial services for the world's underbanked or unbanked population.

DeFi

Designed to handle large and complex DApps such as Ethereum, which currently has a dominance in the DeFi space, but the number of restrictions on this network's infrastructure is increasing. Rates have increased along with Ethereum's market share in DeFi. The growing demand has made it very expensive to process even the smallest transactions on the Ethereum network.

Cardano acts as a development platform for decentralized applications (DApp), which is equipped with support for smart contracts and a multi-asset ledger. It aims to solve the performance issues of the Ethereum and Bitcoin blockchains.

There are scalability issues affecting the first- and second-generation blockchains, which run on a proof-of-work algorithm, which greatly slows down the speed of the network as nodes have to perform complex calculations to reach consensus. The Visa network can process around 65,000 transactions per second, compared to 15 for Ethereum and 7 for Bitcoin. This makes these blockchains too expensive for everyday use and hinders the general acceptance of cryptocurrencies as a means of payment.

Faced with interoperability challenges and sustainability issues that many cryptocurrencies suffer from, especially Bitcoin and Ethereum; Cardano proposes interesting solutions and contributions of importance, given that users cannot use Bitcoin on Ethereum-based DeFi protocols, neither can they make a return of their Bitcoin. The lack of available liquidity leads to difficulties in obtaining loans and high price variations between assets, causing problems for lending platforms, decentralized exchanges and other DeFi applications.

After a malware attack robbed the Ethereum community of a huge amount of funds, the network forked, resulting in Ethereum Classic. Before they could adapt to the new network size, both networks had trouble processing transactions in a timely manner.

Cardano is working on a solution to equip blockchains with an effective governance system. This starts with establishing a secure method for suggesting improvements. The ultimate goal is to make the Cardano network a completely self-sufficient system. In the Shelley era of cryptocurrency, a system was created to reward network participants for staking their ADA tokens in Cardano's liquidity pools. Likewise, the final era, Voltaire, aims to allow the same subscribers to enhance or manage the network.

An innovative coordination and funding mechanism, that's what IOG plans to introduce as a voting mechanism that will allow users to use ADA as a vote to determine how the network will evolve in the future. They will make and vote on suggestions to improve the network. The IOG will establish a pooled development fund to finance improvement proposals. With each transaction on the Cardano network, part of the transaction fees will flow into the fund. In this way, Cardano can become a completely self-sufficient network and achieve complete decentralization. Once the community has control over it, IOG no longer needs to intervene.

IOG approached Wave Financial for help in finding suitable investment opportunities. Within an early-stage process, Wave launched cFund, a crypto-native shelter resource. Wave is character-ized by investing in those projects that promise innovation that will guarantee an acceleration in the development of the Cardano network. Wave evaluates numerous companies that have applied for investment in which cFund could decide to invest, considering the possibilities of synergy with Cardano.

cFund's general partner has extensive experience as founder and managing partner of Wavemaker Partners, which manages USD 470 million in a portfolio of over 350 companies. Thanks to IOG's extensive network, excellent reputation and numerous resources, cFund is able to gain access to unique opportunities. Finally, cFund is backed by an exceptional research tool that plays a key role in finding potential investments. IOG and Wave can conduct a thorough technical review of opportunities, identify companies that meet industry needs, and spot trends early on as active participants in the Blockchain industry.

Testing and demonstrations

Cardano DeFi's Spores project Spores has successfully raised USD 2.3 million in an unprecedented funding round. Cardano-based NFT and DeFi platform Spores raised a significant sum from industry investors.

Spores Network is a new creator-centric NFT and DeFi platform, which starred in a very productive funding round with happy and effective completion.

Spores is Cardano's first full-stack DeFi platform Day by day, Spores strives to increase and develop its game, with a view to becoming the benchmark and number one full-stack NFT and DeFi platform to be incorporated with the Cardano Blockchain. In doing so it seeks to further increase the reach of the rapidly growing NFT market to mainstream users. Lower transaction fees, environmentally friendly transaction processes, higher throughput and a large loyal community will be necessary.

Referring to its funding, Spores Network CEO Duc Luu made it known that at Spores Network there is an intense sense of commitment and ownership after launching its perspective as an NFT and

DeFi backed with global-class crypto VCs and KOLs, seeing a frictionless, boundary-less, creator-equidistant and community-driven becoming of events to create, exchange and communicate work in physical and digital life.

Cardano's Spores aspires to become the Alibaba of the crypto world, this being its ultimate goal to follow, creating an interoperable cross-chain NFT platform that will allow users to not only issue NFT, but also auction and exchange assets, as well as seamlessly use various other DeFi products.

Luu made reference to the fact that the platform has the strongest intention to launch innovative decentralized financial tools that will make it a DeFi giant in the cryptocurrency industry. The project will build Asia's leading NFT marketplace along with other decentralized financing tools to be the Alibaba and Alipay of the crypto world.

The marketplace, according to Spores CEO, will bring creative verticals including digital art, gaming, animation, celebrity and e-sports, while rewarding creators with revenue share and voice.

The funding was backed by industry investors including NGC, SVC, ExNetwork, Focus Labs and Twin Apex, among others.

NGC founding partner Roger Lim let Spores know that the growing interest in non-fungible tokens as a new asset class within the crypto space being a stupendous occasion that those who inhabit, decide to invest; becoming holders of their own digital lives.

At present we see how a variety of executable programs are already in the hands of users who from the network have begun to receive benefits and rewards, thanks to their active participation in sports, art and digital games; receiving their contributions in cryptocurrencies with which they begin to participate in online transactions and negotiations with active, effective and secure presence. This is a different, novel and creative way to see how it is possible to produce and generate electronic money, which would be transferred to your account or wallet in your favorite or most useful token, according to your own particular needs.

On this route and on this path, Cardano undertakes its march or race against time and in front of a varied and dynamic ecosystem, which demands through its users and followers proposals and answers loaded with novelty and reliable updates that are optimal, safe and reliable. It is part of Cardano's commitment and mission, in order to strengthen its DeFi developments.

ZyCrypto is a new DeFi protocol that has been built on the Cardano network. ADAX is an automated market maker that serves Cardano network users with the objective of revolutionizing transactions.

The project was created to enable traders to seamlessly transact on the Cardano network. ADAX is on its way to becoming a powerful trading platform with its facilitation of trust-less token exchange, broader re-routing and non-fungible token (NFT) trading.

ADAX, itself is a mechanized liquidity protocol, making trading more viable and simple in an indisputably decentralized manner without any safeguards as far as the Cardano ecosystem is concerned. ADAX does not have an order book, which helps reduce transaction and network transaction costs. Their website states in one of its parts that:

They have removed all middlemen, complexity and cumbersome procedures from the equation, giving users the freedom to trade without censorship or loss of control over their assets. All those who make life on the network are able to take full control of their tokens, being free to provide their keys, thus ensuring that all their orders are recorded, while they are on a centralized exchange.

Considering that the well-known DeFi protocols could be ignored because of their security structure, ADAX provides full security for its users. This will be facilitated by the DEX imposed by Cardano, which offers secure and fast operations. To encourage greater user participation in the liquidity provision process, resulting in a more dynamic DEX, all exchange fees generated are shared between market makers and liquidity providers.

The protocol is a combined effort of qualified experts from various crypto initiatives. The team behind the project will ensure the success of the project by guaranteeing industry best practices and maximum user benefits.

Despite being based on Cardano, the native ADAX token, ADAX USD is an ERC20 token. ADAX tokens have a total supply of 100,000,000, with only 40% allocated for public distribution.

ADAX chose Cardano because it is expected to become the new standard for cryptocurrencies. Investors recognize the network's potential to challenge the embedded Status Quo of monopolistic and bureaucratic power structures within the cryptocurrency world.

Cardano has changed the Blockchain space through some of the most cutting edge projects. Run by a non-profit organization, the project boasts unmatched security, significantly lower transaction fees and blistering Blockchain speeds.

ADAX's preference for Cardano has accelerated its development in conjunction with Cardano's new features. In the process of promoting in favor of Cardano Smart Contracts, in the third quarter, ADAX will make it easier to participate, bringing liquidity security within the marketplace, to traditional token exchanges by accessing users the maximum benefit within the capabilities and powers of the network.

ADAX plans and projects include the launch of a powerful awareness campaign in favor of the Public IEO brand, in contribution with the Cardano Foundation.

Cardax: A Cardano-based decentralized exchanges project

Since the inception of digital trading assets, most crypto transactions go through centralized trust-based exchanges. However, in recent years, we have seen some interesting innovations in terms of trading technologies within the Blockchain space.

One such innovation is the concept of decentralized exchanges (DEX), which allow traders to find their peers and transact directly on the blockchain. Through DEX, counter-parties eliminate their dependence on centralized trading exchanges and associated custody risks, such as theft or hacking.

The number of decentralized exchanges has increased in recent years. For example, in the Ethereum family, there is Uniswap,

Airswap Protocol, Etherex, IDEX and more. When it comes to the Cardano ecosystem, there is still no decentralized exchange. Tokens created on Cardano do not have a native exchange to list on. To solve this problem, a team of developers has submitted a Fund 4 proposal on Project Catalyst. They are seeking funding of $50,000 to develop Cardax, which will serve as the first DEX in the Cardano ecosystem.

Behind the Cardax project proposal is Ryan Morrison, who leads the team at Quant Digital, a Cardano-based company. Ryan, who is an experienced marketer, stakeholder operator and entrepreneur, believes his team is well equipped with the technical and marketing expertise to make the project a success. The team is composed of developers and cryptocurrency enthusiasts with a deep under-standing of native assets, smart contracts in Cardano and the Blockchain ecosystem in general. Some similar projects the team has worked on include Celsius, Open Ocean and Bitcoin EU.

Taking a somewhat closer look at the roadmap for the Cardax project, a decentralized exchange that will be powered by the Extended Automated Market Maker (EAMM) protocol, we give with the goal of providing liquidity to projects issuing native tokens on Cardano. Following the activation of Mary's hard fork on the Cardano mainnet, which brought native tokens and multi-asset support to Cardano, there is a greater need to develop a native exchange. In addition, with the upcoming launch of the Goguen era, smart contracts will enable the development of decentralized applications on Cardano.

These are great developments that will open up exciting use cases for Cardano at the enterprise level. Having a native Cardano exchange will address some business challenges and gaps within the ecosystem.

SOME FEATURES and capabilities that Cardax will bring to the Cardano network include:

- Support for any native Cardano token.
- Ability to join liquidity pools to collect fees on native ADA-Cardano token pairs.
- Automated liquidity-sensitive pricing using the EAMM protocol
- Ability to exchange ADA for any native Cardano token
- Ability to trade between native Cardano tokens through a single transaction
- Ability to trade and transfer to a different address in a single transaction
- Easy purchase of ADA or any Cardano native token from Yoroi wallet

ACCORDING TO THE PROPOSAL, Ryan and his team are looking to implement this project in six major phases, which a next opportunity and chapter, we will be able to elaborate on extensively with all its details.

Decentralized exchanges (DEX) generally rely on an order book or Automated Market Maker (AMM) to provide market prices. The order book model works best when the exchange offers highly liquid trading pairs, such as BTC/ETH. Most centralized exchanges, such as Binance and Coinbase, use order books. Some decentralized exchanges such as IDEX also use the order book model. However, in markets with low liquidity, order books do not work as well. Users can place orders, but finding a match will not be as easy, so they may end up waiting a long time. As such, they will not escape the volatility and large spreads that occur in these situations.

On the other hand, an automated Market Maker model, such as the one used in Uniswap, is suited to exchanges that offer pairs with low liquidity. The proponent team has been investigating how they can leverage the two models to provide the best trading experience on tokens to be served on Cardax. By combining the best of both worlds, they seek to develop a system that:

- Enable users to become market makers by either starting a liquidity pool or participating in an existing pool.
- Minimize slippage.
- Minimize the risk of temporary loss.
- Provide more price transparency.
- Allow token issuers to create a new pair without having large capital as collateral.

What the future of digital asset exchange holds.

While centralized exchanges provide unique benefits, for now, the shift to decentralized crypto exchanges is necessary for users to realize the full potential of Blockchain. This also aligns with the principles of decentralization and self-sovereignty, which are the key ethos of Blockchain technology.

Thanks to the growing valuable acceptance for Cardano and based on the active decisions that underpin DeFi, a DEX inspired and founded on Cardano, will fulfill a prominent role as an overriding negotiator and power broker within the network. Cardax is set to provide a trusted way to connect stakeholders while promoting equitable governance and participation in the Cardano community. However, as with other decentralized platforms, DEXs are still in their early years and will need further infrastructure development, user experience refinement and improved scaling mechanisms to ensure future adoption.

Few seasoned analysts would argue that decentralized finance (DeFi) has been on a rough road of late. Inconsistent rate swings, a plethora of market fixes and creative ruin have been suppressing those novice, hence more fragile, participants in the area, on par with the strengthening leadership of the more knowledgeable. In addition, KICK.IO, a decentralized fundraising platform based on the Cardano network, has seen a huge opportunity during the chaos.

Although Ethereum, the DeFi industry giant, appears to be on the verge of being laid off, KICK.IO is happy to help.

Although Ethereum continues to benefit from the incumbent's advantages, i.e.; traders are sticking with it for convenience, experts are eager to point out that the current quo will not last. Overall, Cardano, dubbed the "Ethereum Killer," is expected to soon surpass Ethereum in terms of total transactions on the network.

All of this is motivated by inhabiting a great deal of angst with the Proof of Work (PoW) assent procedure within Ethereum, who has allowed a high number of complaints and dissatisfactions with the languid operating rates on the network and otherwise very costly figures. Recently, Ethereum has also come under questioning for its actions before the environmental spectrum, as the most knowledgeable in the matter have opined about the energy incompetence for the development of its processes, which could occasionally transform into a center negative comments, as well as an insurrection of its shareholders.

The trader is and we see it in the frequent search for those legitimate adversaries in favor of the determined specialist, in just as the DeFi market becomes more yearning and environmentally sensitive. Cardano, which was instituted by Charles Hoskinson, who was likewise a co-founder of Ethereum, is the most feasible choice to adjudge itself DeFi's guiding contiguous commitment. Motivated to its own decentralized nature and elevation, it turns out to be quite feasible that the first multi-layered Blockchain in the crypto universe, will generate great brand.

In its own Proof-of-Stake (PoS) protocol, Ouroboros, is categorized as a technological phenomenon. The beginning is being defined by Cardano, about which there is no doubt; with a novel era in transactions and procedures demonstrably very effective, fast, with very low fees and offering cryptographic operations without carbon emissions, with only the use of academic foundations.

KICK.IO's basic and main objective is to lead this transition, providing the opportunity for the DeFi sector to impact changes in its orientation towards the Cardano network. The KICK.IO platform is expected to become a destination where the greater Cardano community can come together to fund high-growth initiatives and choose the champions of tomorrow. KICK.IO is configured to run market-leading functionality, including full Cardano native token support, as well as a set of project startup and backing capabilities that all advanced projects require to move forward and thrive.

KICK.IO is managed by a team of traditional and DeFi financial professionals. With the firm intention of supporting the interests of its parties, KICK.IO processes the exclusive eligibility of honest, competent and reliable projects; those that meet the best potential and standard capable of making a significant contribution to the Cardano ecosystem.

With the Cardano bull market gaining momentum, now is the time to prove that the DeFi sector is still alive and kicking. The invitation is to continue to learn more every day, the fascinating world of decentralized finance or DeFi, a revolutionary ecosystem that every moment is gaining more and more importance throughout the global financial ecosystem, and that has meant the generation of novel economic schemes, of total Blockchain application and usability.

Decentralized Finance DeFi, is the trend that is defining a great commercial activity that is revolving around Blockchain technology on a daily basis, within the network.

Decentralized finance - DeFi specifically seeks to develop traditional tiny financial pieces with extra degree of crispness and decentralization. These small fragments, like Lego pieces, are perfectly combinable with each other, with the firm purpose of extending to a whole financial environment of small solutions that, as a global whole, constitute a major solution for economies that repeal the need for centralized and opaque financial establishments that no longer provide the value expected by the community.

CARDANO'S PRICE EVOLUTION AND WHY IT HAS CREATED SO MANY MILLIONAIRES THIS 2021

The Swiss cryptocurrency Cardano - ADA, witnessed a price increase of almost 100 percent in seven days in early February 2021, amid high investor interest. One reason for this interest is the digital currency's close relationship with Ethereum, as he mathematician Charles Hoskinson co-founded both virtual currencies. In addition, like Ethereum, ADA has an open source format, which means that anyone can further develop this currency.

Cardano continues to soar unstoppably with full power in the third position. Each day has become a new "all-time high" as the cryptocurrency continues a rally that has taken place over the past few months.

The question for many is, what is Cardano doing to do so well?

The crypto is attracting additional interest from traders thanks to its rally. This is as a result to the large trading volume for ADA, which in turn has been generating the rise in its price.

But that's not the only thing driving ADA higher. Cryptocurrency traders are also waiting for a new software update for the network. This is extremely important, because the update should allow it to better compete against bigger rivals, such as Bitcoin and Ethereum mainly, its closest rival; to call it that.

This update will introduce the long-awaited smart contracts that open up an immense range of utilities to Cardano. According to the most recent news, this update should be launched by September 12, 2021.

There are also other reasons why cryptocurrency enthusiasts have taken a liking to ADA. That includes its resilience during cryptocurrency crashes, as well as its low energy usage compared to Bitcoin.

With Cardano hitting a new all-time high, we have to wonder how well the cryptocurrency has fared. Honestly, amazingly. Since the beginning of the year, ADA has gained nearly 1,300%. That makes it one of the best in the crypto spectrum and definitely one of the biggest altcoins to consider. ADA has experienced rises of up to more than 20% in periods of just 24 hours of trading. Of course, Cardano's new all-time high is not the only crypto news worth commenting on.

From being a lesser-known cryptocurrency, Cardano ADA has become the third largest after its price rose to an all-time high that surpassed Binance's native token, according to market valuation.

Some analysts and cryptocurrency enthusiasts had feared that the big new U.S. infrastructure bill would include new regulations that made it more difficult or less profitable to trade cryptocurrencies, but that doesn't appear to be happening. With that potential risk factor seemingly out of the way, cryptocurrencies have been making big gains lately.

In addition to the overall bullish sentiment in the cryptocurrency space, Cardano is also enjoying positive momentum ahead of ADA's listing on Japanese cryptocurrency exchanges, which will take place at the end of August 2021. ADA also appears to be generating excitement ahead of a pending upgrade to be implemented in September and pave the way for smart contracts on the Cardano blockchain.

As we have reiterated, Cardano now has a market cap of approximately in excess of USD 88 billion. Its ADA token is now up approximately 1,420% year to date, and the gains have propelled it to the third largest cryptocurrency by market cap, behind only Ethereum and Bitcoin.

The crypto universe, has been engaged in a fascinating period of growth and great momentum during the last few weeks of the current month of August especially; with Cardano reaching 126% upside throughout its journey, while the number one coin, Bitcoin grows by an estimated 52%, with Ethereum per token at 62% elevation in price.

Predicting pricing action for Cardano and the cryptocurrency market in general involves a great deal of speculation, but there are some potentially important catalysts for ADA on the horizon. In particular, the upcoming upgrade fork that will pave the way for smart contract functionality and other decentralized finance features is definitely an event to watch for.

In this article we represent very personal opinions based on diverse references issued by experts, which may generate certain discrepancies which imbues it with interest and greater desire to contribute to the ecosystem and crypto world so in vogue. Questioning helps us all to think critically about investing and make decisions that help us to be smarter, happier and richer.

Trading volume in Cardano's ADA cryptocurrency increased dramatically just a few days ago while this paper was being written on August 20, propelling the cryptocurrency to a 10% gain in a matter of hours. Cardano, which became the world's third-largest cryptocurrency last week, has seen its price rise by more than 150% in recent weeks.

A little-known digital token linked to the Cardano blockchain has just surpassed other major altcoins to become the world's third largest virtual currency, as network developers aim to capitalize on the rise of decentralized finance that has spread across the globe.

Currently, the popular alternative currency trades on cryptocurrency exchanges such as CoinSwitch Kuber, Cardano's native currency, ADA, defied a major price drop warning to rise to an all-time high, surpassing the previous record. For the first time, the ADA / USD exchange rate surpassed 2.56, marking the culmination of a 154.54% price increase that began on July 20. This was achieved despite renowned trader Peter Brandt's warning of a price drop, which was predicated on a typical bearish pattern known as a head and shoulders pattern.

ADA has been representing significant growth in its price, rising around 50% in just one week, reflecting a clear bullish confidence that recent technological advances will open up Cardano payment systems well ahead of the anticipated September 12 date.

This will enable its network to provide profitable returns. Services such as DeFi, where Ethereum currently holds a dominant position.

In anticipation of Alonzo's planned upgrade, which is scheduled to be released on September 12, ADA investors continue to increase the value of Cardano. The Alonzo upgrade will bring Cardano's ability to handle smart contracts, self-executing agreements between buyers and sellers. The token has consistently gained as Ethereum, Cardano's main competitor, continues to dominate the growing 100 billion USD decentralized financial sector.

Cardano will be able to establish itself as a perfect and genuine player in the spectrum of decentralized DeFi economies, motivated to the effectiveness of smart contracts in favor of Blockchains.

ADA is among the most sought after cryptocurrencies for new traders due to its still relatively low price and excellent marketing as one of the potential Ethereum Killers. There are very few reasons to take into consideration and define Cardano as the preferred coin of the network, and among them ADA is among the most sought-after cryptocurrencies for new users, driven by its good price and encouraging future.

When people use decentralized finance, also known as DeFi, they are transferring financial functions directly to digital ledgers, allowing them to do things like, lend or borrow cash and collect interest on a savings account, all without the need for traditional intermediaries like banks. Its growing prevalence is part of a broader trend of increasing Blockchain usage, which is becoming more and more widespread.

A series of recent surges in cryptocurrencies such as Bitcoin, Ether, ADA and other tokens pushed the cryptocurrency market past USD 2 trillion in value for the first time since the mid-May crash.

With a 1,300% gain in just one year, ADA is among the top five best performing cryptocurrencies, outperforming gains of 1,030% for Binance Coin, 330% for Ether and 59% for Bitcoin, among other cryptocurrencies. On another note, it is worth mentioning that the token is considered highly fragile in the market, given the high volatility of large digital currencies.

In response to RBI's 2018 crypto contention, the value of ADA suffered a heavy drop, estimated at 90% of its value, which established the beginnings of a markedly downward trending market years for younger sector knowledge. However, with the emergence of popular crypto exchanges in India, investments in crypto assets increased from USD 200 million in 2019 to USD 40 billion a year later. As of now, CoinSwitch Kuber, India's leading crypto exchange has more than 9 million registered users invested in crypto.

Let's rest assured that, at the current moments, all eyes will be on the upcoming Alonzo update on September 12 and how it will relate to ADA's current positive streak. If the whole process goes on track, as is to be expected under the current situation; ADA could position itself as Ethereum's number one competitor, and thus ushering in a new era in the cryptocurrency sector.

While the cryptocurrency market in general took a pause, a

breather, Cardano's ADA extended an impressive week-long rally very recently, reaching a 10% rise just in a matter of a few hours in just as much as the level of transactions in the token, consolidated as the world's third most important cryptocurrency; which grew within an evolution of a nearby software modernization that would propel it to give battle to Ethereum.

A KEY PRECEDENT

CARDANO'S ADA soared in May after billionaire Elon Musk soured on Bitcoin and said Tesla would no longer accept the cryptocurrency due to the heavy environmental downside of the huge amounts of electricity used to mine new coins. The fall of the crypto market was so shocking, that there is still no recovery at all in the face of this severe blow. However, ADA rises to new highs as people eager to invest rally en masse for tokens that are more reasonable and effective for the environmental system. Hoskinson has claimed that Cardano uses only 6 gigawatt hours of energy per year, not even 0.01% of the estimated 115.85 Tera watt hours consumed and used by Bitcoin. The token plummeted nearly 60% when the broader market collapsed in the middle of this year 2021, but has since begun to outperform Bitcoin and Ether.

An amazing fact, and one that draws powerful attention within the entire crypto world's pertaining and participating community, is that ADA has soared 1,300% this year alone, making it one of the largest and most important cryptocurrencies within the top five in position and best profitability, compared to top five returns of 1,030% for Binance, 330% for Ether and 59% for Bitcoin. However, the token is also highly susceptible to massive volatility in the broader crypto market.

ADA plummeted nearly 90% in less than two months in early 2018 as regulatory crackdowns on cryptocurrencies ushered in a years-long bear market for the booming, nascent digital industry.

Cardano's meteoric rise over the past three months is catching the attention of some of the most savvy cryptocurrency investors.

Another reason for Cardano's rise is, as mentioned above; its listing on the Japanese stock exchange. The Japanese criteria for entering the market is considered one of the strictest in the world, which is another resounding victory for Cardano. It is worth noting, and it is known to the community; which both Bitcoin, Ethereum and Litecoin are also listed on the Japanese market. Cardano is humbly popular, this because its proof-of-stake blockchain model is considered much more environmentally friendly than any other conventional cryptocurrency.

Proof-of-stake means that coins are randomly allocated to users, which reduces the energy required for a transaction. In contrast, Bitcoin and Ethereum use a proof-of-work mechanism that sees a global network of computers running simultaneously to facilitate a transaction. This procedure requires a high amount of energy consumption, and Bitcoinenergyconsumption.com estimates that Bitcoin generated an amount of 57 million tons of CO_2 in just the average year, an amount that only compares to what a small European country such as Belgium, the Netherlands or Luxembourg can consume.

Billionaire Michael Novogratz sought to gather information on the digital token, also known as ADA, asking for help to explain the more than six-fold increase since mid-December that briefly made it the third-largest cryptocurrency by market value after stalwarts Bitcoin. and Ethereum.

Novogratz isn't alone in asking what's going on with a network that still lacks many features available on its more established rivals. That hasn't stopped it from developing a loyal following on Reddit, similar to many of the so-called meme stocks that surged earlier this year. Unlike GameStop Corp, Cardano has been able to maintain its upward momentum.

Why is it being said that Cardano could outperform Ethereum?

Cardano was tipped to outperform Ethereum, the second largest cryptocurrency in the crypto system. A cryptocurrency that mostly came from being very low-key, is already and on the right track to take out the number two position and potentially even push Bitcoin out of its top spot. Cardano is seen as a cryptocurrency that seemingly came out of nowhere, and today we see it hovering with strong airs of confidence on a very secure and precise path, in which it could well overtake the number two on the list Ethereum in the race, starting to unsettle Bitcoin, the number one in the digital market.

Confidence is building around Cardano, a blockchain invented and disseminated in 2015, after it overtook Binance to take third place on the cryptocurrency ladder, behind Bitcoin and Ethereum. Experts believe that the coin has set its sights or goal on surpassing Ethereum.

According to crypto data manager CoinGecko, Cardano has continued to skyrocket unstoppably, increasing in value and market capitalization. Cardano surpasses in just one month, a growth and rise of its currency, by more than 180%. Cardano's newfound popularity is believed to be due to the announcement of its new, upcoming, major and long-awaited network upgrade called the Alonzo hard fork along with its foray into the Japanese exchange, as just a couple of possible options. The coin's more environmentally friendly processing capabilities and its debut in the Japanese market add considerably to this fervor.

Independent crypto analyst and YouTuber Lark Davis said that, if Cardano quadruples in value, which is frankly possible given its current gains, it would reach the same market cap as Ethereum, even; it would surpass them. And if it were to increase 10 times, then it would be neck and neck with the largest cryptocurrency in history, Bitcoin.

Apparently, it gives the impression that there was something like a "Crypto Battle". A silent fight from which we could see the possibility of finding ourselves with a virtual currency, taking over

Ethereum and Bitcoin. We talk about Cardano and how it has been on an unstoppable march to the top of the crypto network.

Cardano has experienced a fabulous streak this year 2021, despite the fact that the cryptocurrency market has presented certain problems much more recently. Numerous investors are wondering on a daily basis and in the face of these results whether Cardano could ever outperform both Ethereum and Bitcoin.

There is one big plus point that sets Cardano apart from Ethereum and Bitcoin; and that is its well-known environmentally friendly and environmentally committed operation.

According to Hoskinson, Cardano, his creation uses only six gigawatt hours of energy per year.

Meanwhile, Bitcoin and Ethereum run on a combined 180 Tera watt hours per year. Particularly, one Tera watt is equal to 1000 gigawatts, which represents that the energy consumption in parallel with Cardano is significantly higher.

Cardano's test participation system or program limits the number of connectors at the time of testing transactions. This is an operational capability that optimizes the maintenance of comparatively low power. In addition, Cardano processes up to 257 transactions per second, compared to about five and 15 for Bitcoin and Ethereum, respectively.

ARE THERE RISKS?

WHETHER YOU'RE MINING CARDANO, Bitcoin or Ethereum, all of these cryptocurrencies carry risks. This is because they are unregulated, which means you will have no protection if something were to go wrong. Added to this, the amounts and credits easily become very high compared to the market for properly regulated investment items. Thus, a lot of money could be made extremely quickly, in connection with the high volatility in the crypto spectrum. For example, the price of Cardano fell to a low of 1.06USD in May, down from its high of 2.46USD in early August (2021).

Can Cardano outperform Bitcoin and Ethereum?

While Cardano has some advantages, it is still far less valuable than the other two cryptocurrencies. In terms of market capitalization, Cardano is valued at less than 88 billion USD. Bitcoin has a market cap of almost 1 trillion USD, while Ethereum is valued at around 372 billion USD. However, the profitability and profit generated by Cardano, experienced in the last and most recent period of the year, has reached figures higher than Bitcoin's and Ethereum's creases. To date in 2018, Cardano has managed to rise more than 1,400%, Ethereum manages to reach levels of 330% and Bitcoin, at the tip of the iceberg is up 67%. Given this, we raise a question:

Is it able to sustain such a level of profits in the long term?

Take into account the words of the renowned YouTuber, Lark Davis, who, in his framework as a cryptanalyst, expressed in his digital channel that, given the possibility that Cardano quadruples its value, which could easily happen; it would equal its market capitalization on par with Ethereum. And if it were to increase 10 times, then it would have the same limit as Bitcoin. Meanwhile, another expert is skeptical about big gains for Cardano in the long run.

"Cardano is a vessel in a rising blockchain and broader DLT tide," Elizabeth Hunker, an advisor at blockchain firm DecentraNET, told The Sun. "But its longevity and/or long-term lunar potential is another thing entirely, and entirely dependent on whether its Ghost Chain ecosystem, aka the notable lack of dApps, this would make sense and come to life." By the end of 2010, experts are confident and expect Cardano to reach 5USD, according to Coin Price Forecast. Then, by mid-2025, Cardano's price is expected to double to 10USD. This would give it an implacable market capitalization of approximately 316 billion USD.

In one year, WalletInvestor forecasts Cardano's price to hover around 4.74USD. In five years, the forecast rises to approximately 12.51USD. On the other hand, Tesla CEO Elon Musk, who is sometimes influential on market trends, has expressed environmental concerns about Bitcoin. The price of Bitcoin has been volatile since Musk said Tesla in May would stop accepting payments represented in this cryptocurrency. However, Musk still owns Bitcoin and has said there is a future with the cryptocurrency and Tesla. The billionaire also owns Ethereum, but not Cardano.

WHY HAS it been said and popularized that Cardano could be the "Ethereum killer"?

THE CARDANO-ETHEREUM RACE IS A MARATHON, not a sprint or sprinting effort. Cardano and Ethereum have a lot in common. Both are types of digital currencies that also function as programmable ecosystems. That means that other digital currencies and applications can be built on their networks. These cryptocurrencies are in turn traveling toward the same endpoint. But they are taking very different routes and approaches.

The main man behind Ethereum is Vitalik Buterin. Cardano was launched by Charles Hoskinson, who also co-founded Ethereum. Both are well respected in the cryptocurrency industry.

Ethereum was launched two years before Cardano, and it started doing very well. It is developing its technology as it goes along and is currently implementing a much-needed Ethereum 2.0 upgrade in stages. In contrast, every step Cardano takes is reviewed by experts. This thorough testing means it developed much slower than Ethereum.

Cardano calls itself a third-generation blockchain. It wants to solve some of the scalability and other problems faced by Ethereum and Bitcoin. Instead of placing solutions on top of existing technology, it started from scratch and built an entirely new Blockchain.

There are two important factors that have to be taken very well into account. Two concepts illustrate the different challenges Ethereum and Cardano are facing right now: smart contracts and proof of stake.

RECAP: Smart contracts.

SMALL PIECES of self-executing code that live on the blockchain. Without smart contracts, the blockchain can only record transactions. With them, you can actually execute agreements. For example, you may be able to take out a smart insurance policy that automatically pays out when certain conditions are met. Smart contracts are the secret sauce behind non-fungible tokens (NFTs) and decentralized apps (Dapps).

Ethereum is winning the smart contract race. Not only does it have smart contracts enabled, but more than 2,800 decentralized applications are also using its network. According to State of the Dapps, about 80% of Dapps are running on the Ethereum network.

In contrast, Cardano is testing its smart contract capabilities right now and expects to fully launch in September 2021.

Proof of participation Without getting too technical, blockchains are sophisticated databases that don't need a third party to authenticate data. They secure themselves. But, for them to work, they need a process to validate transactions and make sure no one tries to cheat the system.

Bitcoin and Ethereum do this through a mining system called "proof of work." This has been criticized recently for its high power consumption. And, while it is super secure, it is also slower and more expensive than other ways of validating transactions. Proof-of-participation is a popular alternative to proof-of-work. It limits the amount of energy consumed by the coin and is faster and cheaper.

Cardano was designed to use proof of stake from the beginning. It is a green cryptocurrency that uses a fraction of the energy of

Ethereum and Bitcoin and will be able to process around 1 million transactions per second. Once it launches, Ethereum 2.0 will be able to process about 100,000 transactions per second and will use 99.95% less energy than it does today. To put those transaction speeds in context, Visa processes about 1,700 transactions per second.

So I'll let you in on the secret, could Cardano overtake Ethereum?

THIS YEAR 2021 is crucial for the Cardano-Ethereum race. Cardano plans to launch smart contracts and Ethereum will move to a proof-of-stake model. Much depends on whether both can do so without technical problems.

Ethereum's first mover advantage cannot be overstated. Even if Cardano's technology ultimately turns out to be superior, it won't mean much if people don't use it. Cardano may be comfortable playing the long game, but it won't reach the end of its technical roadmap until at least 2025. And four years is a long time in such a rapidly developing cryptocurrency industry.

However, Ethereum is congested and transactions are expensive right now. Some developers have already moved away from Ethereum due to network congestion. It will be interesting to see how many more do so before the proof-of-stake update is rolled out. Especially since there are several other players in the market that already have smart contracts enabled. The Ethereum 2.0 upgrade has been in the works for some time, and the switch to proof-of-stake will not be easy.

Cardano has the potential to eventually overtake Ethereum. It's the difference between re-paving or widening an existing road and building an entirely new road. But there's no reason Ethereum and Cardano can't coexist and even work with each other.

Cardano is focused on ways Blockchain can solve real problems in developing countries. It recently announced a major partnership with the Ethiopian Ministry of Education. Ethereum has its eyes on economic applications. For example, Visa is using the Ethereum network to settle crypto transactions.

With such different visions, there is a good chance that both will become successful Blockchain ecosystems in their own right. And if the market for Blockchain solutions continues to grow, there will be plenty of room for both.

Cardano, a Blockchain platform powered by the ADA coin, has been the subject of a lot of buzz in the cryptocurrency world recently, with some staunch advocates going so far as to call the platform the next "Ethereum Killer." However, Cardano has some serious short-comings that serve to highlight the platform's persistent underdog characterization.

For those who are not yet part of the cryptographic process, it is worth noting that Cardano is a crypto operated and managed by a non-profit foundation, which interacts closely with academia for the exploration and improvement of most of the aspects that constitute the Blockchain platform. ADA is Cardano's own coin, "first third-generation crypto", capable of providing resolution to the problem in the scalability dilemma, relative to coins representing generations before or prior to Cardano, including Bitcoin and Ethereum.

Bitcoin received enough criticism recently for the exorbitant power consumption of its network. At the heart of this problem is Bitcoin's Proof of Work mining mechanism, where miners spend computational power performing cryptographic calculations to have the occasion to legalize a given transaction for further processing on the Blockchain. In addition, each and every transaction must be replicated in each and every node: computerized equipment that processes Bitcoin execution software and accumulates the entire Blockchain.

Unlike Bitcoin, Cardano's Ouroboros algorithm uses a proof-of-stake authentication mechanism in which a collection of nodes is run by a leader that validates transactions and then incorporates those transactions into the Cardano blockchain.

Now, Blockchain network scalability is something that all cryptocurrencies have to deal with. The Bitcoin Lightning network aims to increase the processing power of the world's largest cryptocurrency by adding another layer to the Bitcoin ecosystem, which gives greater speed to transaction processing by bypassing the Blockchain, thus, allowing Bitcoins to be transmitted between wallets immediately and free of pooled fees. Of course, closing credit for a number of bilateral transactions on the Lightning Network still required registration on the Bitcoin Blockchain.

In the same way that Cardano has been doing, Ethereum is activated in a move aimed at a Proof of Stake module. Ethereum 2.0, expected to be fully implemented by the end of 2022, will incorporate two fundamental changes: fragmentation and participation.

Under fragmentation, the Ethereum blockchain will be split into distinct "fragments." All of these fragments will behave just like a standalone Blockchain, making room for its own Smart Contract blocks and transaction validators.

Similarly, to shape a deal within the network, those fulfilling the role of "miners" for Ethereum 2.0 will simply place bets or lock themselves by blockchain to a certain and determinate amount of Ether within the master nodes. The incentive for such transaction processing will be distributed according to the amount of Ether that has been staked by an authenticator. These are two major changes that will certainly increase the processing power within the Ethereum network to more than 100,000 transactions every second and, at the same time, will forcefully compress a particular brand of power.

This brings us to the heart of the matter. Every relevant update to the Cardano network is peer-reviewed, ensuring optimal system performance. In addition, Cardano is also excelling in the transaction processing power race. A simple example, the layer 2 scaling resolution in the network, also distinguished as Hydra, would increase its processing power by up to 1 million transactions per second.

This means that Cardano could process 10 times more transactions than those processed by Ethereum 2.0. Despite this, Ethereum stands to win the competition for Smart Contracts and dApps, applications processed behind a point decentralized computing system such as a Blockchain. While Cardano is expected to release smart contract functionality, known as the Alonzo update, Ethereum already features 2,822 dAps, corresponding to 78.3 percent of the entire ecosystem.

Although Cardano has an advantage in terms of transaction processing power, it would be very difficult (for the blockchain to emerge) to usurp Ethereum's first mover advantage in relation to smart contracts and dApps. Consequently, I don't think Cardano is about to become an "Ethereum Killer" anytime soon.

Of course, as we have witnessed throughout this year during the meme stock saga, hype is a very potent force. And Cardano seems to be getting a lot of hype thanks to ADA's 894 percent gain so far this year. In contrast, Ethereum's Ether coin has posted a much more modest 217 percent gain over the same time period. If this kind of weighting were to hold, dApp developers would come to perceive a high enough reward to start targeting Cardano with a forceful attitude and determination, thus progressively dispensing with the competitive superiority represented by Ethereum.

A SELECTION OF CARDANO'S BEST PROJECTS FROM WHICH YOU CAN EARN HIGH RETURNS

I n its constant dynamic of training, preparation and execution, by its multidisciplinary training team, Cardano ADA, has seen and is aware of the need and requires its wonderful cryptographic platform; since it seeks a palpable presence and 100% consistent and participatory, giving the opportunity to its own crypto community, to build from its own development programs, projects of change that will drive it in a tireless marathon with vision to maintain and exceed its position as the third best digital currency in the world.

Cardano - ADA, according to its creator Charles Hoskinson, currently has more than 100 commercial projects to its credit.

IOG CEO Charles Hoskinson noted a few months ago already,

that its third-generation Blockchain platform, Cardano - ADA, has more than 100 commercial projects in the pipeline.

Its native Cardano token, ADA; has been printing significant price performance since the beginning of the year. We have been able to appreciate how ADA has been trading with significant progressive increases in its trading price in the market.

Moreover, according to CoinMarketCap, ADA has recorded a price increase of over 400% year to date. This superb performance raises questions as to what could have started the positive trend.

In its portfolio, Cardano now has more than 100 commercial development projects in its pipeline. Charles Hoskinson said that the fundamental value of the project has always been evident, and that at the moment there are just over 100 major commercial operating participatory projects being structured for Cardano. Hoskinson said that, at this very moment, I have for Cardano; an inventory of over 100 commercial projects in the pipeline that want to migrate or build directly from Cardano now.

As Herald Sheets previously made known, SingularityNET (AGI), an Artificial Intelligence (AI) solution built on the Ethereum blockchain, has begun its second phase of migration to the Cardano blockchain. That seems to be a good start, as the community is awaiting the Goguen.

According to IOG, this will be the first major token release on the smart contract platform. At the same time, it is the largest democratic exercise in the history of decentralized Artificial Intelligence (AI). As the IOG chief rightly put it, these stakeholders are not limited to decentralized finance (DeFi) protocols and crypto projects. For his part Hoskinson emphasized that, in Cardano, you have Fortune 500 interests as well as large government interests.

John O'Connor, IOG's Director of African Operations, announced that Cardano ADA is on the verge of securing a contract with an African government. Although development progress is yet to be disclosed, the Blockchain project is optimistic of welcoming millions of users to the fast-growing Cardano ecosystem for real-world use.

The decentralized cryptocurrency network founded by Hoskinson, which aims to lead the DeFi space by developing partnerships on the African continent. The organizers of the Blockchain Africa Conference 2021 made an announcement about Charles Hoskinson, founder and CEO of IOG and inventor of Cardano, who delivered a speech on "Cardano Development Projects on the African Continent."

Hoskinson also announced at the Blockchain Africa Conference that Cardano was close to agreements and initiatives. He admired the demographics of Africa, specifically in Ethiopia, where the number of inhabitants as of January 1, 2021 is 21.45 billion. Hoskinson said the DeFi sector would gain close to 100 million users over the next three years by tapping into the potential of the developing country market.

In a discussion of Cardano's use case in Africa, Charles Hoskinson spoke in reference to the implementation plan for Cardano's smart contract support during the "Cardano360" virtual conference, revealing late last year that the company was working on a number of development projects involving Cardano that are aimed exclusively at Africa.

With respect to South Africa, Cardano is working on a project focused on insurance identity for millions in the densely populated country; it is estimated that 100 million users may be brought on board in the first stage. The views expressed on FXStreet are those of the individual authors and do not necessarily represent the views of FXStreet or its management. As for resistance, speculators will find a lower amount between 1.25USD and 1.27USD before the heavens open.

Charles Hoskinson, CEO of IOHK and head of the Cardano blockchain, recently revealed in a YouTube video that the company's long-term development focus will rely primarily on Africa. Africa has long been an ignored economic bloc despite its enormous potential.

In 2019, IOHK partner Emurgo published about SMART Africa, an initiative to unite all African countries into a single digital marketplace, which ADA could execute. Cardano's efforts in Africa are wide-ranging. In a new video titled "Reflections on Roadmap," the IOHK (Input Output Hong Kong) Global CEO shared how ADA plans to scale in Africa: "We are going to increase resources there to eight figures, as very good news is coming." FXStreet will not accept liability for any loss or damage, including without limitation to, any loss of profit, which may arise directly or indirectly from the use of or reliance on such information. ADA Pools data shows that, in total, more than 22.2 billion Cardano has been wagered.

With Africa being the continent with the second highest demographic index in the world, this could make it the future leading region for decentralized finance. If you decide to trade currencies, it is appropriate that you first consider very carefully; what are those investment objectives you have in mind, what is your level of experience and the real identification of your appetite for risk. It is important to keep in mind that you are reading a set of opinions and views that do not necessarily reflect FX Street's own policy or official position or those of related organizations.

Regarding their project development in Africa, Hoskinson only asks for a little patience and assures that they are leveraging Atala Prism to implement an identity solution for the unbanked in Africa.

Charles Hoskinson, made it known that IOHK has sent an official request to the Cardano Foundation board to establish a clear and concise strategy for Africa and Japan. Cardano's ADA token managed to extend to the rally that has made it one of the best performing crypto-assets of the year, helped by the excitement surrounding the upcoming listing of Coinbase shares on Nasdaq. In the past, Charles Hoskinson, has spoken of the enormous potential of the African continent for the adaptation of Blockchain technology, about which he has great confidence and excellent expectations.

The high degree of leverage can work against it as well as for it. Speaking at the Blockchain Africa Conference, CEO of IOHK, Charles Hoskinson revealed a bullish news, about the roadmap. Hoskinson shared that IOHK (Input Output Hong Kong) Global intends to scale in size around the world, with a focus on growing its business in Africa. Cardano has more than 100 commercial projects in the pipeline, Hoskinson says.

Cardano has had a strong existence in Africa for years; its team is exploring expanding into other African countries with plans to establish a laboratory. The organization must do its own thorough research before making any investment decisions. IOHK, the company behind Cardano, is one of the few companies actively working in Africa.

IOHK's Director of African Operations, John O'Connor, announced that Cardano is on the verge of securing a contract with the Ethiopian government in Africa. COTI has received 500,000USD from cFund, marking the first investment made by the Cardano-backed venture fund, the network behind today's third largest cryptocurrency. Cardano - ADA, could well be linked to Africa's future, as Hoskinson revealed. IOG opened its first office in Africa in Ethiopia two years after the start of the construction of the Cardano protocol.

Cardano's founder, is updating the crypto community on the company's plans to expand operations. On Africa's digital focus, it is an extremely young continent with a strong focus on digital developments. Many experts speculate around the news of Cardano Africa, leading them to believe that it has to do with the implementation of Blockchain technology in the agricultural ecosystem through fertilizer vouchers and other land services and jobs.

It is also working in 5 more countries including Kenya, Nigeria, South Africa, Tanzania and Ethiopia. After building local relationships, training staff and overcoming obstacles, the platform would be at a tipping point within the continent. But, without the go-ahead from the other side, Cardano is obliged to keep the details of its developments under wraps for the time being.

Now, using a standard definition of a measured move, ADA could reach 5.50USD and easily position it as one of the most prominent cryptocurrencies by market capitalization. IOHK, is one of the few companies actively working in Africa. Its presence requires investment in building digital infrastructures such as optical networks, data centers and satellites.

There are several regions in Africa that will be able to rely on a real-world blockchain solution that will provide the necessary infrastructure to ensure a wide reach, just like the prospects on Smart Africa and Tanzania. With this, currency trading outside of the

Cardano protocol brings with it a high level of expertise and countries with an appetite for risk, considering development projects that will hopefully be established in laboratory of agreements and initiatives through its participatory audience.

Africa is at the center-point for Cardano's injection, incursion, planning and development in favor of a region considered of great importance for its expansion from a digital economic point of view, with the implementation of Cardano ADA in the region, great changes of greatness will affect only in a positive way.

What is so special about the more than 100 Cardano projects under development?

Cardano ADA, has become the most discussed topic in the cryptocurrency world today, as its rapidly emerging alternative currency ADA token ranks among the top three cryptos in the world. With a very high potential, Cardano has attracted investors' potential, while market analysts are optimistic about the coin.

Driving this intense growth of Cardano's blockchain, recently its CEO Charles Hoskinson said that the company is currently involved in more than 100 projects it is working on. Commenting on Cardano's extensive growth in a recent interview, he said, "I have over a hundred commercial projects in the pipeline that want to migrate or build something on Cardano."

CoinMarketCap's data on Cardano is fascinating to hear, as it says Cardano has gained over 400% from last year to date. Moreover, with these 100+ projects in the works, one can expect nothing but an uptick in its honest growth.

WHAT ARE these 100+ projects?

OF COURSE, Cardano has not yet revealed all of its 100+ projects, but ideas were given about some of them. These projects may have the potential to revolutionize the crypto-sphere and, at the same time, speculation arises as to whether they will all be implemented first.

An artificial intelligence (AI) solution SingularityNET (AGI) recently revealed that it has engaged with Cardano to continue its second phase of migration to the Cardano blockchain. This is one of the projects that Hoskinson said has been in the pipeline.

SingularityNET announced that it would create one billion new AGI tokens on the Cardano blockchain. According to IOHK, this will be the first major token launch on the Cardano Native Assets platform and is the largest democratic exercise in the history of decentralized AI.

Commenting further on the project, Cardano developers stated that this will be the highest democratic exercise in AI and the first major token to be launched on the smart contract platform.

In addition to the aforementioned project, there will be projects encompassing cryptocurrencies and decentralized finance (DeFi) protocols, according to Hoskinson. He said that the government, as well as Fortune 500 companies, are interested in these projects, having interest in Fortune 500 and interest in government.

Cardano's interest in Africa

Cardano's CEO highlighted the fact that there are many opportunities available in emerging African markets and those opportunities need to be executed well. In his statement on government interest, he was referring to that of African governments.

During the second week of last February, IOHK's director of African operations, John O'Connor, announced that Cardano is on the verge of securing a contract with the Ethiopian government in Africa. But he did not specify about the level of development of the project.

This can be seen as a sign that the platform has opened its arms to welcome various partnerships and other projects that want to use Cardano's platform to expand their products.

Expectations regarding Goguen

As time goes by, expectations continue to grow about the next major major upgrade that Cardano's network will have. Known as "The era of Goguen", which would bring with it the possibility of operating Smart Contracts on its Blockchain, opening the way for decentralized applications (Dapps) and diverse possibilities of use.

Among the multiple aspects that tend to found the highest rate of expectations and hopes regarding Cardano, is the technological support in favor of digital assets represented in other networks, such as the probability of migrating to new projects developed in different programming languages, as is the case of Solidity; to start decentralized network procedures.

Meanwhile, Cardano's ADA token, has capitalized significant gains, increasing in important percentages in recent times.

Price prediction ADA Cardano had a massive rally in 2021 and remained in a daily uptrend despite recent liquidation. Now, after ADA bulls held a key support level, Cardano is poised for a new leg up, potentially to new all-time highs above 1.48USD. According to FXStreet appreciations in its price forecast.

According to CoinPedia, Cardano will realize its highest value increase throughout the year and could record a new all-time high. By the end of 2021, it projects the possibility that ADA could reach 10.00USD, with the start of a 2022 with a price hovering around 12.00USD being likely.

New projects for Cardano could be a game changer Cardano's native token, ADA, has increased over 700% in value this year, reaching over 2.50USD in real and otherwise expected value. Moreover, NFTs generated a lot of buzz and the craze surrounding them is no less attractive and interesting.

Recognized as a cryptocurrency trader, Lark Davis has had the courage to predict a whole array of totally categorical cryptocurrency opinions, promising his initial investors, relevant returns not seen in this process.

The Cardano blockchain development team has already revealed new information about the smart contract launch. Following the launch of its Mary protocol in March, Charles Hoskinson's Cardano has announced that its Alonzo update will be available by next September.

The addition of smart contracts to Cardano would result in a flood of startups, which could reward investors and thus create new revenue opportunities.

According to Lark Davis, smart contracts will hit the mainnet for Cardano probably in September, assuming there are no delays with their Roadmap, so we are about to see this fair explosion of new projects coming to Cardano in just a matter of days from the date.

Definitely, Elrond decided to publish his first snapshot of Maiar Exchange, finding himself similarly on Davis' radar. All this will give the first EGLD charts a chance to see how their MEX governance token funds are growing. With the highest number of tokens spread across EGLD, the MEX governance token will give the group the opportunity to make certain decisions. And also the launch of its fundraising mechanism, launch pad on the blockchain, which represents another great value for the token.

ACCORDING TO DAVIS, **the Elrond launch pad will introduce a new wave of tokens to the Elrond universe.**

FOR DAVIS, entry is being made to large Solana (SOL) events, all motivated to its large turnover, attractive rates and dimensions. Solana itself, it is decided to build from itself, as the ecosystem becomes a wider world; without falling into compromises of high censorship. Considering that Solana's own assets remain optimistic, this will not be what will become its biggest profits.

The well-known Non Fungible Tokens (NFT), which represent exclusive digital assets, widely used to display digital art, box office, real estate and much more, represent a wonderful trend that, for the YouTuber, will continue to give benefits to the many investors.

For Davis, NFTs represent a powerful value proposition within the recreational (gaming) market of the crypto world, in which these virtual assets are bought on a daily basis, sold and also traded; in the same way as in the sports industry, in which every digital card or collectible piece tends to be quite common.

Within the multiple development plans, Cardano will have first Big Data project after a significant investment of 3.4 million USD.

IAGON will start developing the first Big Data platform on the Cardano Blockchain. The startup will develop a fully decentralized cloud storage platform. Meanwhile, the ADA token continues to increase its value day after day, gradually; holding on to its privileged third place as the best digital currency in the world.

Through a significant number of investors, the startup on par with its technology, has been enabled through multiple investors, the tech startup has managed to generate the resources required for self-management of its plans, these ready to be executed on the Cardano network. Navjit Dhaliwal, who has the privilege of being the founder of IAGON, celebrated such scope and expressed that thanks to the support received in the crypto world, everything will be ready to offer a true and recognized decentralized option in favor of computational demands in the cloud, such as Amazon Web Services (AWS) and other technologies usable in Big Tech today.

Understanding the IAGON development project IAGON is progressing towards a decentralized cloud platform that will allow access to information and records in any environment and at any time, with the proposed increased security and consistency of cloud services. In addition, all new and upcoming hosts will be able to benefit from special rates and exclusive storage capacity on the network.

IAGON's business consultant, Darren Camas, commented on how information in the cloud has changed the cost structure of data storage, highlighting the company's philosophy of creating a market-place of distributed and decentralized computing resources through Cardano's Blockchain.

At the same time, on the other hand, the Big Data project is totally impractical on other Blockchain such as Ethereum, due to high network commission costs.

ADA price movements The ADA token, native to the Cardano network, had one of the best performances seen in the crypto market in recent months. The cryptocurrency has an appreciation of over 1,600% compared to July last year, according to data from CoinGecko.

Close to what will be the new and future updates of the Cardano Blockchain, which will feature stablecoins, Smart Contracts and NFT, as well as partnerships with governmental entities and private companies, ADA reached an all-time high of 2.55USD for the month of August this year (Time of writing).

Despite the general declines observed in recent weeks in the crypto market, ADA managed to remain among the top five cryptocurrencies with the highest value in the market.

Some developments available on Cardano, input from its own community.

CARDANO WALL:

Demonstrates various use cases of transaction data. It can sign messages and create proofs of existence for files.

CRYPTO MAGE:

This game focuses on amazing mages who create magic, increase their skills, find totems, learn crafts, complete quests and much more.

DAEDALUS:

Daedalus is a full node and developed by IOHK, one of the founding entities of Cardano.

GIMBALABS:

Gimbalabs is a collaborative community and a space where

dApps and OpenSource tools are developed in the "Playground" (Project Based Learning Experiences). Everyone is welcome to join every Tuesday at 4 p.m. UTC!

NFT MAKER:

Create your own NFT by uploading an image and paying an ADA.

NOWPAYMENTS:

Payment gateway provider for accepting ADA payments and ADA donations.

POOLTOOL MOBILE:

Explore Cardano, track your rewards and receive notifications to take action on certain events.

H.Y.P.E. SKULLS:

A new level of collectible NFT is coming to the Cardano network! 1,500 unique 3D animated cards with the HYPE skull. No two are alike. Always handmade. Never automated. Transaction Meta

DATA BROWSER:

Browse and search for different types of transaction metadata in Cardano.

THE IMPORTANCE of ADA as a Development Project in favor of the Cardano ecosystem.

. . .

CARDANO, the first third-generation blockchain to emerge from an early research approach, uses ADA as its native cryptocurrency token. Although ADA is at the core of the Cardano ecosystem, the reason for its existence may not always be clear.

For Cardano insiders and insiders, it is important to understand the purpose of this cryptocurrency.

WHY IS ADA IMPORTANT, and what is it needed for?

LET'S look at a few main reasons why ADA is critical to the Cardano ecosystem and how EMURGO is building products to support a developed Cardano ADA ecosystem.

First, you need ADA to bet. Stake exists because Cardano is a proof-of-stake (PoS) blockchain. To understand how this works in a simple way, we previously used the example of a supermarket. In a supermarket, there are several checkouts. Each checkout is manned by a cashier. These cashiers scan baskets of goods and the cashiers are rewarded with cash or assets for doing so.

Within Cardano, each cashier is an interest group operator. Each payment is an interest group. A basket of goods is a group of transactions that are grouped into a block, which are added to the Cardano blockchain permanently once they are scanned by cashiers and validated as correct. Within the Cardano supermarket, there is space to support 1,000 cashiers and checkouts. These cashiers will need to use special equipment to operate a checkout 24/7 and keep Cardano's blockchain up to date. The Cardano blockchain is a supermarket that never closes.

However, not every ADA owner will want to run a checkout. Some people will want to help run checkouts without starting one. That's why it's important to gamble. Regular, everyday Cardano users can delegate their ADA resources (their stake) in certain boxes. This allows cashiers to expand their checkouts to a healthy size and increase their chances of a customer with a basket of products visiting their checkout. For their efforts, cashiers (stakeholder opera-tors) are rewarded with ADA.

Without this reward, hard working cashiers would quit and the Cardano blockchain would not be able to continue. For people who bet their resources or coins on these payments, they also get a reward. This means that people get ADA for betting as an incentive mechanism.

CARDANO **ADA** ALLOWS **transfers of value**

AFTER BEING REWARDED WITH ADA, cashiers have the right to transfer or retain it as they wish. Cashiers or share group operators, people assisting cashiers, share delegates and anyone else who owns ADA are entitled to transfer value to anyone with an ADA address. The ADA holder simply needs to know the public address of the person to whom they are sending value, just like sending value to an email address.

There are many examples of transfers of value that could occur. Recently, Emurgo brought cryptocurrencies using ADA through Yoroi ADA Wallet developed by Emurgo to Japanese comedian Kenji Tamura's famous restaurant, "Charcoal Grill BBQ Tamura". This means that anyone can pay for a menu item with some ADA. There are many other examples of merchants, restaurants and retail outlets that have accepted ADA as a form of payment, including Emurho's ADA Crypto Card campaign that successfully sold out in South Korea earlier this year.

Emurgo constantly updates Yoroi Wallet for Android, iOS, Chrome and Firefox to make ADA transfer a seamless, simple and secure experience for all users. It is a free and essential tool devel-oped for users to store, send and receive ADA, allowing Yoroi Wallet to be the financial gateway to the future.

In addition, Emurgo is also supporting Syre from Cardano Fellow Robert Kornacki through its dLab / Emurgo accelerator program.

Syre is a pioneering tokenless invoice-based protocol designed to make ADA remittance easy and worry-free for users by eliminating any concerns about confirming recipient ADA wallet addresses, and will be applicable to Cardano ADA in addition to other blockchains.

CARDANO ADA WILL BE NEEDED for smart contracts

SMART CONTRACTS ARE a planned feature of Cardano in the near future. Every purchase or transaction we make every day tells a story. Some stories are simple. One might be the story of a person buying their morning coffee. Another story might be a mortgage or loan payment. These stories are more complex.

Each story needs a script. This means creating a meaningful set of rules and guidelines that allow transfers of value to take place. Smart contracts write the necessary scripts for these stories. Cardano's ADAs will be the actors in the script. This is the third reason ADA exists. In early April 2019, Emurgo announced the development of Seiza, a Cardano blockchain explorer with new features, which was subsequently released for public use in May 2019.

Seiza will allow users to track their ADA transactions and other vital Cardano blockchain-related information, including wallet histories, addresses, block size and interest groups, among others. This essential Cardano ADA product will become increasingly important as Cardano moves towards full decentralization with participation, stakeholders and increased ADA liquidity.

Cardano ADA a treasure with freedom

In a democratic system, every person has a voice. This voice allows a person to vote to elect officials, change laws and have a say in how their country operates. This democratic system is decentralized by nature. In true democracy, choices are made through fair elections that are held on a nationwide basis, which should not be alienated by some influential individual. Those who own or are interested in ADA would be like its citizens, those who would give life to the Cardano network.

This means that all stakeholders have a voice. If each person who owns ADA acts in his or her own self-interest, he or she will want what improves Cardano as a whole. This will make Cardano more valuable as a public blockchain. This would be similar to citizens voting for officials who promise to improve a country's roads and waterways. These improvements benefit everyone.

Cardano improvements will one day be funded by a treasury and are important to the sustainability of the Cardano ecosystem. This means that the ADA will be entrusted to parties working for the betterment of the ecosystem, as voted for by the citizens of Cardano, the holders of the ADA.

While the role of ADA is not always clear at first glance, there are a number of core functions that the native cryptocurrency plays in the Cardano ecosystem. There is no single reason for ADA, however, it is timely to lay out key pillars that explain the purpose of ADA along with Emurgo's strategies to support the Cardano ADA ecosystem with product development.

At the same time, with the dawn of Shelley comes the future era of a fully decentralized Cardano. This era will usher in many new opportunities, allowing anyone to help participate in keeping the Cardano blockchain decentralized. The phases of Cardano's development can be clearly seen in the Cardano Roadmap, a cryptocurrency that is filled with power.

GENERATING PASSIVE INCOME WITH CARDANO (ADA) USING OTHER CRYPTOCURRENCIES

As you may have noticed throughout the development of the book, currently there are several ways to generate money with cryptocurrencies, there are many opportunities. While there are some that are more risky (and depend on your ability) such as trading, DeFi platforms, etc, there are others that are more recommended and less risky, such as Hodl (hold) of a cryptocurrency and wait for its price to rise, although this earning model is absolutely passive and speculative, as it is a long-term strategy, we have other strategies that can also help you generate passive income, as is the strategy that I will present below.

This strategy has existed for many years, it is widely used by banks today, although in a higher percentage of profit, this is to generate interest with your assets.

In the world of cryptocurrencies this modality already exists and is led by one of the most reliable companies in the environment: BlockFi, which is backed by the Gemini exchange and people as recognized in the environment as Anthony Pompliano.

BlockFi allows us to transfer our funds to the platform and generate an annual interest that goes from 6% (for cryptocurrencies such as Bitcoin) or almost 10% with stablecoins (which are cryptocurrencies that are 1 to 1 with the dollar, such as USDT and USDC to name a few).

If you are interested in this modality, you can open a BlockFi account at the following link and earn $250 worth of Bitcoin for free:

Get your BONUS on BlockFi here

IN CASE you are reading this book in print version you can scan the following QR code with your cell phone:

THE MOST IMPORTANT THINGS TO KEEP IN MIND WITH CARDANO

T o conclude this book, I would like to thank you for taking the time to read it, I wanted to clarify a few things before finishing.

Many people have tried dabbling in cryptocurrencies, some with success others with moderate results, but all with results in the end, the important thing is that you keep in mind that the cryptocurrency market is a highly manipulated market, which is why I recommend that you always pay attention to the indicators that you can see in TradingView, see the signals it sends you, continue learning about trading, if you are interested you can dedicate yourself to them, but if not you can dedicate yourself to do HODL (the meaning of this within the Cryptocurrencies is related to buy coins when there is a significant decline (for example if Bitcoin is at \$58000 and drops to \$36500 that's where you buy and go buying as it goes down, never when it goes up, this is known as Dollar Cost Averaging is a strategy widely used in the trading environment) and keep those cryptocurrencies for years until they double, triple or quadruple their value, it is not uncommon in the environment, as well have done those early adopters who bought Bitcoin when it was worth \$0.006 cents, did HODL for 14 years and when Bitcoin reached its all-time high of \$20,000 dollars in 2017 and \$60,000 in 2021, sold everything and became millionaires. But as always, choose the method you like best and follow it at your own risk.

Finally, I would like to know your comments to continue to nurture this book and to help many more people, for them would you help us by leaving a review of this book, in order to continue providing great books to you, my readers, which I appreciate very much.

LINKS **for you**

Check crypto prices here:
https://coinmarketcap.com/
Get free Bitcoin:
Get free bitcoin here
Get your BlockFi bonus here:
https://blockfi.com/?ref=76971ae9

Trading crypto:

Binance

Bitmex

Buy Crypto:

Coinbase

CEX.IO

Changally

Localbitcoins

Donde guardar tus criptomonedas:

Get the Trezor Model T here

Get the Trezor Model ONE here

Get a Ledger Nano S here

More trading tools at:

www.TradingView.com

Best regards
Sebastian Andres

DO YOU WANT TO FURTHER DEEPEN YOUR KNOWLEDGE?

I f you found this book very useful, let me tell you that this book is part of the collection "Criptomonedas en Español" where we want to transmit all the current education and information based on the most traded and known cryptocurrencies (the books will be updated every year as progress is made).

- Volume 1: **Bitcoin in a Nutshell**
- Volume 2: **Ethereum in a Nutshell**
- Volume 3: **Dogecoin in a Nutshell**
- Volume 4: **Cardano in a Nutshell**
- Volume 5: **Solana in a Nutshell**

Table of Contents

Introduction: How To Use This Book

Imagine a world where you are walking around with a form of money in your pocket. You want it to grow, and extensively so, but it won't do any good just sitting in your wallet. You don't want to entrust it to a bank either. So you decide to exchange the money for a little chip. This chip is a little risky, but it can grow your money's value, and you can, in turn, receive the profits. The flip to this coin, however, is that it can also reduce in value. There is no set and firm way to truly predict whether or not this chip will turn in your favor. You can exchange these chips with other currencies (such as US dollars or British pounds) and use them as a method to pay for things without having to change the currency.

This is the backbone of cryptocurrency investment. It is a form of exchanging money online to a digital currency that fluctuates. It either increases in value, thus giving you a return on investment, or it decreases. You can hold on to it, sell it, or trade it. It actually doesn't take long to start investing in cryptocurrency. However, as a beginner, it is best not to jump the gun and start investing without acquiring the power of proper knowledge. If you are interested in cryptocurrency but struggle to understand what it is exactly, where to start, and what to look out for, then come along for the ride.

This book will dive in-depth into investments, especially in cryptocurrency and Bitcoin. It starts with a definition and examples, then moves to how you can do proper cryptocurrency investing and what you should expect. We will teach you eight commonly made beginner mistakes and how to avoid them. We simplify complicated concepts such as blockchain and cryptocurrency rules. Scammers and hackers are always a factor whenever working online, regardless of whether you are investing in cryptocurrency or not. Therefore, it is essential to learn what to look out for and remain safe online, especially when large amounts of money are involved. This book also expands into investing in high tech companies. It also gives you a clear understanding of bubbles, the history behind them, and what to watch out for, considering their impact on the investment world and cryptocurrency. Furthermore, it is best to understand the revolution that cryptocurrency might just bring.

Read through the chapters carefully, making sure to understand and grasp all of the more complicated concepts before moving onto the next. It is crucial to understand and remember anything that can help you (and not break you) when investing. Knowledge is power, and it certainly is no different when it comes to trading online. It may feel overwhelming at first, but once you have grasped everything, you will be far more confident in the decisions you make.

In the end, you should walk away with knowledge of the history and how to invest in cryptocurrency and what the future may hold. Once you understand cryptocurrency investing, it is not so daunting or difficult—we arm you with the information you need to know to invest wisely. As risky as it may be, it can be highly rewarding. But here is a piece of advice that will save you a lot of grief and a lot of trouble and pave your journey to success—don't invest any money you cannot afford to lose!

Chapter 1: Understanding Investments

Is investment a solid form of income or a means of speculation with hopes for a good result? Is investment too risky to consider? Can I invest in it at a young age? These are all questions people ask from time to time, yet when asked about the clear definition of investing, they find themselves oddly perplexed. In order to understand cryptocurrency investments, one should understand investments and cryptocurrency separately. In order to grasp investments, it is best to go as far as to define what money is.

According to Merriam-Webster Dictionary (2021), money is something generally accepted as a medium of exchange, a measure of value, or a means of payment.

There are various conjectures about the origins of money, but the diverse reasons were to settle the troubles of bartering, debt, and even to pay wages for people's work. It is not necessary to understand the whole system of money. Still, it is good to know its origins and that money developed differently in different countries, which is why different currencies exist. Money does run at different values. For example, US dollars are different from the European Union's euros, which are different from British pounds and Indian rupees.

So What Is Investing?

Everyone's goal is to grow their source of income (money), and sometimes they deem it best for this growth to happen through passive income (where someone does not have to work for hours on end to earn). Investing can be seen as a form of passive income. Investing, according to Merriam-Webster Dictionary (2021), is defined as "to commit (money) in order to earn a financial return."

In the clearest terms, you can view the investment as trading your money for an object (like a stock or currency) that, over time, will give you money in return. Hopefully, you earn enough to cover your initial investment and earn a profit. You can also invest money in commodities or antiques that will grow in value as they age, and you can sell them to gain a higher amount than your original investment, thus creating a profit for yourself.

On the other side of the spectrum, when someone starts a business or wants to grow their wealth, they often need the financial coverage to do so. Not wanting to place themselves in debt from a bank, they can consider having people invest in their company. Once people start buying in, the owner can use their investment to grow their business and profits and eventually return profits to the investors. However, it also means the person who controls the business has no debt they have to pay off, boosting the business's financial well-being.

What Can I Invest In?

There are various forms and assets in which you can invest. For instance, you can invest in:

- Defensive investments (such as electric utilities)
- Shares (a growing or steady business)
- Property (rental property or real estate)
- Cash (savings accounts or long-term deposits)
- Fixed interest accounts (e.g., treasury bonds)
- Digital assets (Bitcoin, etc.)

This book will look at cryptocurrency investments, a form of digital assets, and also how to invest in high tech companies through shares.

How Do You Start Investing?

First of all, you need to have an income. Investing requires money—whether you already have savings or need to cut out a small cost like a daily drink at the coffee shop so you can put that money away. What you want to invest in can also determine the amount of money you need to start.

Secondly, it is often best to do your own research and look at the facts before even consulting a financial professional. One might think there is no need for expert help, but how are you to assess their ability or even the possibility that they may be a scammer?

Thirdly, you need goals. Set realistic goals which can be monitored, and do not stress too much if things don't always work out. At the same time, it is also wise to form and develop an effective strategy that will open doors for your best chance at success. Take your time, consult with others, and if you don't understand something, do more research.

Once you have discovered what you want to invest in (and you have the money), it is best to open an investment account. With cryptocurrency investments, it is normally a digital wallet (e-wallet). With tech companies, you can open up a brokerage account.

After all your research, and you've saved enough, set your goals, and implemented a solid strategy, you are ready to get started. The sooner you can start to invest, the better. Investments are all about patience and returns. The longer you have been investing, the higher your success and return can be. So you can start at any age, but it is ideal to begin as soon as possible.

Why Invest?

Successful investing builds wealth—the ultimate motive and reason why you should invest. It is best to think about your future, especially retirement, where pension funds may not be enough to cover your basic living expenses. You can reach your financial goals a lot sooner and possibly acquire greater wealth than if you were just relying on your job's salary.

You can also invest in order to grow a business or even help to support others in times of need. Investment often allows you to be a part of supporting a new growing business, which in itself can be rewarding.

Furthermore, passive income sets you up to not only survive in the financial world but also to thrive. Eliminate the time that you need to work and grind and fill it with the goals and dreams you aspire to.

Understanding Passive Investing and Active Investing

Although investments are seen as a form of passive income, it is best to understand that this will not always be the case. Certain forms of investment require great time, care, and work in order to be successful.

- **Active investments**: as 'active' implies, this form of investment normally requires your attention, time, and work. Active investments certainly focus on buying and selling, taking advantage of short-term money fluctuations and educated guesses in order to achieve success and gain a larger income. One acts as a portfolio manager. However, active investments are more expensive and certainly more time-consuming.

- **Passive investments**: require more tracking and less work. Passive investments commonly have long-term goals intertwined with less buying and selling. Passive investments are cheaper and more relaxed. However, this can limit the products you want to invest in, and despite the lower risk, may have a lower return.

Cryptocurrency investments can be both a passive or active form of investment. However, due to cryptocurrency's nature, active investment in this form is normally required. These are all things you have to take into consideration.

General Pros and Cons of Investing

Investing requires less time and action than trading and earning at a traditional job to make money. Being a form of long-term income growth means you can prepare and plan to use it for the future, whether for retirement or to save for your own business. Depending on what you invest in, you can get a high return depending on how your investment works out.

However, investing is generally a risky business, and there is no absolute or certain guarantee that you will get a return on what you put in. There are higher and lower risk investments in general, and investment is normally a slow form of moneymaking. Patience and research are needed. If you invest today, you cannot expect to see immediate results tomorrow. Strategies may not always work. Even if you do as much research and work as possible and set up a highly logical strategy, things can still go wrong.

In life, there are pros and cons to everything. Even drinking coffee has its pros and cons. Therefore, you need to assess whether the rewards are worth the risk. This is especially true when it comes to cryptocurrency investment.

Be an Intelligent Investor

Everyone should strive towards being an intelligent investor. This means practicing the investing principles of patience, risk protection, analysis, and being in control.

Investing is a waiting game. One requires patience and not jumping the gun but rather holding back until the best deal or opportunity comes along. One does not simply ride each wave of excitement or opportunity that might spike every now and then. Instead, they understand the value of taking their time when it comes to making the right decisions.

Investing has risk; therefore, it is best to reduce as much risk as possible by ensuring the money you invest is money you can afford to lose. Don't invest in one target but rather in several in order to ensure that one failure doesn't drain all your money.

Study, research, and then do more research. You can never know too much when it comes to investing. Make sure you know what you are staking your money on, know the risks, and then make a decision. Do not make any decisions on a whim as you are then meddling with luck, not wisdom.

Having self-control and being realistic about your goal is the best way to go about investing. The get-rich-quick schemes are often too risky or are a scam. Play your cards carefully and monitor the rewards you receive. Do not shoot at what you cannot hit—aim carefully at what you can manage both financially and strategically. This is what investment is about. Be sure the reward is worth the risk and ensure that you don't get caught up in investment promises that are too good to be true.

Also remember that in the game of investment, you can't allow yourself to get emotionally involved. It is quite easy to fret and panic at any dips or occasions that may look bleak. However, if you panic and withdraw your investments, it may just cost you a lot more than if you remained patient.

Things You Should Consider Before Investing

When you first step into the world of trading and investing, especially in cryptocurrency, experts and analysts alike highly recommend that you consider paper trading first. Trading, much like anything, is a skill to be honed but has an effective price tag on it. Therefore, any mistakes or blunders made due to being a beginner or lacking in knowledge may cost you immensely. Paper trading can help prevent that.

Paper trading offers you a learning experience that allows you to practice trading online without using money. You can use a variety of simulation applications to read trading charts, draw up strategies, and grow your understanding of cryptocurrency in general. This can help build up your confidence, learn from what normally could be costly mistakes, and develop a specific strategy of your own to test out. Furthermore, with the lowered risk, you won't experience a rampant of high emotions with every decision you make.

Keep in mind, however, that although paper trading does remove the emotional element, it does not prepare you for this when you are trading with real money. It also does not account for any extra fees that come with authentic trading. It is best to keep all these things in mind as you practice paper trading. A simulation can only help prepare you so much, but it will never be quite the same as reality. An airplane simulation is a good example. Many pilots in training spend hours in a computerized cockpit to understand the inner workings of the plane. However, the risk of crashing is removed by the obvious fact they are not flying the real deal, and despite all, a simulator's multiple calculations cannot possibly factor in all the elements that could go wrong.

Practice, then practice some more. A person can never fully master the craft of skating at the rink or riding a horse without dedicating multiple hours. When investing in cryptocurrency, it is best to spend time and effort in order to be successful in the long haul. Whether you take a passive or more hands-on approach to investing in cryptocurrency, don't hesitate to take any opportunity to practice and learn. The better you understand something, the more likely you will be able to identify a successful investment or trading opportunity and avoid the multiple scams that are out there.

You will face very real competition against other traders and investors. Especially as a beginner, you tend to face those who have had more experience for longer. This can have an impact on the shares you sell and trends to watch. Many online brokers allow you to add functions for paper trading, allowing you to improve your skills without experiencing any losses. This not only allows you to hone in trading on a particular platform but also equips you with the knowledge that main experienced traders may have.

There are thousands of people who invest, but not many prepare as they should. Putting in the time and dedication already sets you ahead in the market.

Trading Simulation Apps

When approaching paper trading, you want to get the most out of it. Start off by creating a trading account on one of these simulation platforms. Keep your paper trading scenarios as realistic as possible, aligned to what you can manage in real life. Remember to analyze and study the results of each and every strategy you use. It is also wise to remember that practice versus real life has its differences, and it is almost guaranteed for matters to worsen when you start live trading. Be prepared for this, and lower your expectations even if you think you are applying a brilliant strategy.

In order to train properly, you need to pick an effective and accurate platform in which to hone your skill. Here are some of the top platforms recommended by other traders:

- **StocksToTrade** is a user-friendly simulation app designed by real-life traders, and it is bound to get you on the right route. It offers a realistic practice ground with tools and scans that you can use to your heart's content.
- **TradingView** is good for both beginners and those more advanced in the trading world. It includes great charts and technical analysis that will grow your learning experience.
- **E*Trade** is popular and includes a variety of tools. It can act as a sort of simulation letting you apply new strategies and get relatively accurate results for what may occur in real life.
- **TradeStation** is a good platform to consider if you have had some knowledge of trading in the past. Many experts tend to use this platform, as do people who have moderate knowledge in applying new strategies.

Once you're familiar with paper trading, it is time to get your feet wet with cryptocurrency!

Chapter 2: Understanding Blockchain

When the word blockchain appears, a few images might come to mind, including that of a bunch of LEGO® stacked together, creating a chain. Obviously, this is not the case, and it may seem complicated and daunting when you first come to know of blockchain. However, starting from the beginning and moving forward, you will see that as complex as it is, it is relatively easy to understand.

The concept of blockchain was outlined in 1991 by W. Scott Stornetta and Stuart Haber. The idea behind it was to reduce the risk of hacking or tampering to create a safe and secure system. Twenty years later, it sprung into life with the invention of Bitcoin and has been used in cryptocurrency ever since.

What Is Blockchain?

Blockchain is a way to build trust in businesses. In society today, it is no wonder that deceit and insecurity run rampant on the web, but trust is still needed in order for a business to sell, and yet, that trust is easily breakable. Blockchain was invented to create trust between the client and the seller. In 1992, the initial idea of blockchain was sparked by Stuart Harper and W. Scott Stornetta, whose work was to design blocks of information that were so secure no one could tamper with the data. This idea arose due to mistrust and scams that were running amidst transactions across the world.

To first understand blockchain, you need to know what a ledger is. A ledger is a record of financial transactions. For instance, if you sell and purchase secondhand boats, you would record in a ledger all the purchases you made and keep track of all the clients who paid you and how much they paid. However, it is easy to tamper with ledgers. For example, as a business owner, you could easily modify ledger entries by recording your product as being purchased and sold five times instead of twice. Middlemen such as banks were therefore created to make the dealings formal and legal, and buyers and sellers were no longer solely responsible for the financial records. The centralized middlemen acted as intermediaries between transactions to keep things honest and fair.

In the middle of the Great Depression, the trust in banks had greatly faltered. Due to stock markets crashing and a panic to regain their money, people had suffered great financial loss. A sense of helplessness and distrust formed between the buyers, sellers, and the middlemen over control of assets. As time has gone on, some intermediaries have been known to be biased or corrupt or made mistakes that cost others their money. Meanwhile, buyers and sellers had to rely on an element of blind faith when it came to these middlemen.

This is where blockchain comes into play. Blockchain is a decentralized method of keeping a ledger of transactions which eliminates the middlemen like banks or the government. Because copies of the ledger are stored in multiple locations and a transaction's history is 'chained' together, it makes it easy to spot any form of tampering.

Here is the concept behind blockchain:

- A key is created along with every transaction made and stored into a 'block' of information.
- The record is also stamped by all the nodes (different decentralized computers that run blockchain), creating a singular block of information.
- When a second transaction is made, just like the first one, it also has an unhackable key and is stamped. This second key is 'chained' to the first and also retains a record of the first block's key. When a third transaction comes into play, it repeats the same cycle but now holds onto the key of the second block.
- This carries on in an infinite cycle of ledger information that can be trusted, considering no one can tamper or hack into and change the ledgers.

In technical terms, a blockchain is made up of these blocks of information, but each one has the hash (a special stamp or code) of the ledger entry created prior. Each time a transaction is made, the information is recorded on the block permanently. Therefore, in order to hack into the blockchain, one would have to hack into multiple blocks in order to ensure the special stamp or code matches up with each block. However, to permanently seal the security, there are multiple computer nodes that contain copies of the blockchain. Therefore if any blockchain is tampered with on one computer, the other computers still have the authentic copy. A hack would be pointless as one would have to hack multiple blocks of information across multiple nodes to get a majority "vote" of the participating servers to prove the authenticity of the information. Although tampering could be possible, it is easy to detect, and there is limited time before the information is replaced with the authentic copy.

This is one of the many reasons blockchain has become so vastly popular. In a world where people like to cheat or scam when it comes to money, including cryptocurrency, what better way to avoid this than by developing a technology that is incredibly difficult for cybercriminals to hack? Furthermore, unlike a bank teller or other higher authority that can be bribed or manipulated, blockchain removes this factor entirely. There is no ultimate blockchain authority; rather, it is popular due its decentralization and lack of involvement of the government and banks.

Although blockchain was originally used for the recording of Bitcoin transactions, in this day and age, people can make use of it to transfer other forms of data safely. For example, you may know of the music service streaming service—Spotify. They use blockchain to assist the creators of music to control licenses and get paid in a more direct and simplified way globally via cryptocurrency.

There are multiple businesses that use blockchain, and the better you understand it, the more likely you will succeed when working with cryptocurrency.

Blockchain Terminology to Know

Because blockchain is the foundation of cryptocurrency, you may come across some terminology that will be important for you to get to know and understand.

- **Node:** refers to any computer that is connected to a blockchain network. When a computer is considered as a full node, it means that the computer has the hardware and ability to validate the transactions. However, a light node refers to a computer that can only do a partial amount of work.
- **Distributed Ledger Technology (DLT):** is the general term used to describe the database

that blockchain runs on, spread across nodes for different users to access.

- **Hash:** in simplified terms, it works as the digital fingerprint designed in a blockchain. It is the code or 'key' in a blockchain transaction.
- **Smart Contract**: is used frequently amongst businesses that use cryptocurrency. Smart contracts are like a self-executing contract that works on lines of code. They are relatively new and remove the need for a mediator to be present while a contract is being signed.
- **Fiat currency:** is the form of money issued by the government. Take note that cryptocurrency is not a fiat currency. Secondly, fiat currency is practically unlimited, whereas cryptocurrency is not.
- **Liquidity:** refers to an asset's ability to get converted into cash over a certain period of time. The quicker it is to convert, the higher the liquidity.
- **Peer-to-Peer (P2P):** is normally the interaction that occurs between two parties, normally in regards to the transactions between the buying and selling without a third party (such as a bank being involved).

What Is a Cryptocurrency?

A cryptocurrency is a digital form of money—an online currency which people use to trade and purchase and obviously invest. Many people use blockchain technology in order to keep their transactions and recording of data secure. There are also many conflicting viewpoints on cryptocurrency, both positive and negative.

Cryptocurrencies are the best ways of transferring money anonymously and to avoid centralized methods such as banks. However, they are known to be volatile and still need an element of stability in order to be taken more seriously in the future.

The first cryptocurrency created was Bitcoin in 2009. The startling truth is that no one really knows who designed the system or the currency. Satoshi Nakamoto, a pseudonym for the true designer, also designed the blockchain behind the Bitcoin system. The popularity of Bitcoins has since then exploded, and there are up to 18.6 million Bitcoins in existence. (Hayes, 2021).

In order to buy cryptocurrencies, you will need to download an online e-wallet app. You can then make an account to exchange your money (in your local country's currency) into a cryptocurrency online. When the transactions take place using blockchain technology, the sellers are basically signing off their ownership of their cryptocurrency and sending it to your wallet's address. Therefore, in order to use the cryptocurrency now stored, you will be given a private key that matches the one on the public blockchain's ledger. This private key establishes you as the owner of the coins you bought.

Do be aware that the legality of cryptocurrency may vary from country to country. So before even considering investing in cryptocurrency, make sure the law allows it. It is always best to stay on the legal side, even if it is online. We'll get into much more detail about the legalities in Chapter 4.

Cryptocurrency has its benefits, but it also has its fair share of drawbacks. This is why it is up to you to analyze and assess whether the reward is worth the risk. Let's take a look now at the pros and cons of cryptocurrency.

Pros of Cryptocurrency

- Being anonymous is very handy from time to time, and it is a guarantee while using any cryptocurrency—this allows for peace of mind. You can avoid being a target of theft and build your confidence as an investor.
- Financial transactions can be direct and eliminate the middlemen. It cuts back on time and effort and reduces your risk of intermediaries losing your money.
- You can make immediate purchases within the comfort of your own home.

- Whenever money is transferred between different banks, especially international payments with different currencies, you can rack up hefty transfer fees. With cryptocurrency, there are no transfer fees at all, thus cutting losses significantly.

- It is estimated that about 2.2 billion people have access to the internet, but not to the average services provided by banks. In 2017, only 35% of the African population could access a bank. In 2018, over 191 million people in India still did not have a bank account (Times of India, 2018) . Being on the internet gives you immediate access to cryptocurrency services should you wish.

- With blockchain technology, it dissuades trackers and thieves from trying to tamper with online ledgers. There is a higher element of security in regards to cryptocurrency transactions, and with the blockchain, as we mentioned earlier, copies of your transactions distributed between several computers will prevent fraud and tampering from others. However, as you'll read about in the list of cons, the security isn't perfect.

- When entrusting your assets and money to a bank, you are delivering it to a third party. There is always the potential for errors that may cut off your access to what is rightfully yours. You might have to jump through some major technical and legal issues in order to retrieve your assets. With cryptocurrency, you are the

individual owner, and you hold all the control of your assets.
- Over the rough patch of ten or more years, cryptocurrency, specifically Bitcoin, has started to stabilize.

Cons of Cryptocurrency

- Despite having the high security of blockchain technology to protect your transactions, cybersecurity can still be a major issue. Many people have lost quite a sum of money due to hackers, whether they gain access to your digital e-wallet or through the transfers themselves.
- If you lose or forget your digital e-wallet password, due to the high security necessary to prevent cybercrime, there is no way to retrieve your data. Therefore, losing your password could rack up major losses on your part.
- Due to the varying hourly fluctuations of pricing, cryptocurrency is an unstable method of payment. It could be cheap today and expensive tomorrow; thus, the uncertainty and sense of unpredictability can make it a risky asset to own.
- Because cryptocurrency is decentralized, there is no regulation or control as to how it runs. Despite decentralization being a major advantage, it can also be a major drawback with issues occurring and regulations changing by

the whim. Without rules, there can be a certain element of chaos, enough to spin someone into a whirlwind of either great loss or great gain.

Bitcoin Explained

It is time now to dive deeper into the first cryptocurrency known as Bitcoin. At its core, Bitcoin is a decentralized currency system that removes banks and credit card companies as the central authority. For example, when you make a purchase today using your credit card, it is the credit card company that verifies how much available credit you have and keeps track of your credit card transactions. You put all your trust into the credit card company to manage your transactions. Bitcoin is also a form of digital currency. People use Bitcoin to buy and sell, investing using the pay-and-hold strategy (waiting for Bitcoin's value to grow from the original time it was purchased). The people making the transactions are completely anonymous, which might lead you to believe you can't trust anyone. However, the system of blockchain works as such that you don't always need to!

Bitcoin is a digital, decentralized, anonymous system of transaction ledgers and blockchain ledgers which use private and public keys (passwords) and mathematical equations to keep control of the currency flow. To perform any financial transaction, you need to prove that you have enough money to make the purchase and prove that you've paid for the goods or service. So, how does Bitcoin help with this? Bitcoin uses digital e-wallet software to keep track of account balances and purchase history. When you want to trade goods and services for Bitcoins, you initiate the transaction through your Bitcoin digital e-wallet software. Each transaction gets assigned a specific 'private key' which is a mathematically generated password that belongs only to you and verifies you as the Bitcoin owner. All computer nodes that participate in the Bitcoin network keep a copy of the transaction ledger, which is a record of every transaction that has ever been made with Bitcoins. This transaction ledger is used to verify that you have available funds by comparing your 'private key' against past transactions that have been made using that same key.

The Bitcoin system is anonymous because you don't know who is sending Bitcoins to whom; everything is tracked by keys. Each transaction you make has a unique key; if you ever lose this key, there is no central authority who can reset your 'password.' If you lose your keys offline e-wallet (for example, due to a hard drive failure), your transaction is gone forever.

Bitcoin itself, however, rose to several heights of popularity despite all the risks entailed. During the years 2009-2020, there were many events that shaped the reputation of Bitcoin, which you will need to know in order to fully understand it.

Trading Education (2020) offers a Bitcoin timeline, with all currency indicated in US dollars, as follows:

2009—Bitcoin was launched for the first time.

2010—The popularity of Bitcoin rose when its value grew from having no value to $0.39 per Bitcoin during the year.

2011—Competition arose to start combating against Bitcoin, whose value rose from $1 to $31 but hurtled down to a shocking $2 by the end of the year.

2012—Bitcoin started to place its foot in the door on a global scale. It started at $4 and ended up with its value at $13 by the end of the year

2013—This was the crucial year of Bitcoin, having firmly placed its foothold in the online market. Due to financial issues in Europe and the major lack of trust in banks, many investors turned to Bitcoin to place their assets in, similar to a mini gold rush. This resulted in the rise of value for Bitcoin, which grew from $260 to $1,000 but fell back to $750 by the end of the year. Bitcoin started to fluctuate more regarding prices, creating both greater loss and gain in the cryptocurrency world. This largely occurred to its growth spurts in popularity (higher demand with limited stock increasing its value), but due to scams and government regulations, its value declined as people started to sell it just as quickly, deeming it less valuable.

2014—Mt. Gox, the largest Bitcoin currency exchange at the time, declared bankruptcy after experiencing tremendous loss due to cybercrime. Throughout the remainder of the year, Bitcoin had a bit of a rough patch with the rise of cybercrime, fraudsters, and scams. China had forbidden Bitcoin, and news quickly spread, which also had a massive negative impact on this cryptocurrency.

2015—After a huge downhill slide, Bitcoin reached a level playing field in stabilizing. Investors started to grow an interest in this platform again. Even banks started to use Bitcoin because they wanted to take part in its growth. It stretched to a total value of $360 per Bitcoin by the end of the year.

2016—Bitcoin rose to an estimated value of $1,000 this year, considering Japan had accepted it as a form of currency, and the demand exploded.

2017—This year was the ultimate boom for Bitcoin, where it jumped to a value of almost $20,000 per coin. This had a mind-blowing impact on the financial world, and Bitcoin sealed its permanent residency and popularity on the web. No one truly knows why it blew up so exponentially on the market, but again, there are a few speculations.

2018—It seemed Bitcoin had reached the peak; it had a massive slide downhill in 2018, where it decreased in value to $3,500 by the end of November. This caused massive losses and again stamped its reputation of being a volatile investment.

2019—Bitcoin had a steady and sturdy climb upwards again, reaching the amount of $10,000 per coin once again due to steady growth in popularity and value.

2020—With a global pandemic, 2020 was a maze of uncertainty for Bitcoin, where it brought a blow to cryptocurrency when the value of Bitcoin fell by half. However, it made some point of recovery and was valued at $20,000 again by the end of the year. This is in and of itself a surprising turn.

Taking a Look at Bitcoin Mining

Now that you have a basic understanding of blockchain and Bitcoin, let's take a deeper look at *Bitcoin mining* which is a common term in the cryptocurrency world. A Bitcoin miner is the name for the person who is running Bitcoin mining software on a computer in order to validate Bitcoin transactions. They ensure that all the transactions are true and have not been tampered with. This role has to exist in the digital currency world because there is no central authority to ensure that the person buying a good or service using Bitcoins actually has the actual required amount of Bitcoin available. This is known as the "double-spend" problem, where buyers try to use the same Bitcoin to spend on different items online. These miners check or ensure that users don't spend a certain Bitcoin more than once. Due to the time delays with Bitcoin transactions, it is quite possible to pull this off, but this is where Bitcoin miners come into play. Although with blockchain technology, it is very easy to see whether or not an item has been tampered with, someone needs to actually double-check the Bitcoin transactions.

Much like "gold" mining, a Bitcoin miner digs through complex puzzles and finds blocks of transactions that have indeed been verified. In return, they are rewarded through payment in cryptocurrency. In its most simplistic form, Bitcoin miners use high-powered computer hardware and software to perform a similar role to what bank tellers do: verifying your identity and that you have available funds. As miners verify transactions, they are given certain digital "time slots" in which they can update the Bitcoin public blockchain ledger with this information. This ensures that all computers participating in the Bitcoin network have the same information via the central ledger. Once miners have discovered 1 MB worth of transactions, they are eligible for a Bitcoin reward, but it does not necessarily mean they will always receive it due to competition from other miners. Furthermore, with the fluctuating cryptocurrency, even if you have received a reward it may not pay out as much in the end.

Pros and Cons of Bitcoin Mining

Pros:

- Bitcoin mining has its rewards, especially with the ability to earn money for the work that you have managed from the comfort of your own home.
- Mining is more profitable these days because the number of miners has actually dropped. As a result, problem-solving is becoming easier, and miners don't have to fight against so many competitors.
- Cloud mining has given an advantage to people who do not have the computer processing power to work on normal Bitcoin mining platforms. You now have the ability to hire or rent the necessary processing power and time in order to compete in mining. Just open an account, choose your desired computational processing power (called a hash rate), cover the hosting fees, and let the mining begin!
- Any hardware you purchase for mining will remain valuable long after you decide to stop with the mining.
- You are also assisting with the growth of the cryptocurrency market, playing a role in the digital financial world. Cryptocurrency only works when a large group of people decides to use it.

Cons:

- Learning to mine Bitcoin is not easy, and it might also be very difficult to ensure all your equipment is set up and running smoothly.

- The hardware necessary to mine has a heavy impact on the use of electricity which may have some major consequences on your bill.
- There is no shortage of scammers, and this, unfortunately, includes Bitcoin mining.
- Mining does not necessarily guarantee the money; therefore, in the long term, you might end up running at a loss.

Pros and Cons of Bitcoin Investing

Now that both the definition of Bitcoin and its inner workings have been covered, it is now time to assess and learn the benefits and risks of investing in Bitcoin.

Considering Bitcoin is the first of its kind, it is running ahead in popularity and value. Furthermore, despite its major ups and downs, it has made it this far. Bitcoin is far ahead of its competitors, making it by far the best in the field.

After going through a brief summary of the history of Bitcoin, you can understand how volatile and fluctuating investing in Bitcoin can be. Some people have had massive success while others have plummeted hard. It is all a level of risk, and that is why you never invest what you cannot afford to lose. The rewards may be great, but being wise with the loss will guarantee you success in the long run. We'll take a look now at the pros and cons of investing in Bitcoin.

Pros of Bitcoin Investment

- Whether you want to invest at midnight or at one in the afternoon, crypto investing is always available 24/7, unlike banks that have lineups and only open and closed at specific times.
- Being able to work and invest from the comfort of your own home is a major advantage.
- Bitcoin is a liquid asset or known by reputation to be one. You can invest in Bitcoin both long and short term, and you can easily trade it at a moment's notice.
- At times, return on investments from Bitcoin have been bigger than in many other investment options. Therefore, it is good to assess whether the risk is indeed worth the reward.

Cons of Bitcoin investment

- Bitcoin can also be a little slow in the transaction process, considering the volume of users and transactions made at the same time. This can be a great cause of stress and nerves, especially if you want to make a quick sale.

- Considering Bitcoin is the most popular form of cryptocurrency, it is not a surprise that cybertheft would specifically target it, especially considering it is of higher value than most other cryptocurrencies. Whether it is hacking through e-wallets or fraud, spam, black market sales, or more, much like any form of money, it does have its risks of getting stolen.
- The volatility is also a major downfall of Bitcoin because its lack of predictability turns the currency into a gamble. Truthfully, no one can tell for sure why it is so volatile. There is only speculation of the value rising and falling due to popularity, bad news, and scams. Even a tweet could possibly change the inflation of cryptocurrency!

Ethereum Explained

Bitcoin remains the strongest and most popular form of cryptocurrency in the market at the moment. However, other forms of cryptocurrencies are rising up to the challenge. Online currencies such as Ethereum, Namecoin, Litecoin, and Peercoin are all known as altcoins (coins that were created after Bitcoin).

Now that you have a good understanding of Bitcoin, let's take a deeper look at Ethereum. In 2015, Ethereum was first launched and had its own form of cryptocurrency called Ether. It also runs on blockchain and has no third parties involved. It started a brand new path, working on fixing the general flaws that revealed themselves in the original crypto, Bitcoin.

Ethereum started with two general roles: one was the creation of smart contracts, and the other was for trading cryptocurrency in a secure environment. Despite having its own form of crypto (Ether), it also offers other forms of exchange, such as through smart contracts or Ethereum Virtual Machine (EVM). Ethereum traditionally takes 12 seconds to confirm a transaction in comparison to Bitcoin's average of 10 minutes. There is more potential for miners in Ethereum to earn Ethers than for Bitcoin miners to earn Bitcoin.

However, much like Bitcoin, Ethereum suffered its own hard knocks since it launched. In 2016, about $50 million in Ethers were stolen by a hacker that had people questioning the true security of this cryptocurrency. This resulted in Ethereum being split into two: Ethereum (ETH) and Ethereum Classic (ETC).

In 2017, Ethereum rose at a massive rate of over 13,000%, which attracted many investors and boosted its popularity. However, this sudden growth spurt did make others more cautious of its high volatility rate.

Still young and very much unpredictable, it is hard to say which direction Ethereum will go. Ethereum is the second-largest cryptocurrency up and running, and some of the pros and cons to using it follow.

Pros of Ethereum

- The founder, Vitalik Buterin, is known and popular. This certainly establishes a sense of certainty and credibility that Bitcoin may not necessarily have, considering no one knows who actually designed it.
- The planning and strategies are easier to understand with strong and growing support for the cryptocurrency platform.
- It's drawing in more businesses as it is more than just a cryptocurrency. It offers other services such as decentralized application processing power and the use of smart contracts.
- Ethereum is also much faster and certainly not as limited as Bitcoin can be, therefore making transactions far more convenient.

Cons of Ethereum

- Ethereum is weakened, however, due to the fact that it offers so many platforms. This makes the programs and the coding potentially more vulnerable to problems such as breakdowns, hacks, and other issues online.

- If you are new to Ethereum, it is hard to tackle it as a beginner as there is a lack of training to use this platform. So despite having a general understanding of how it works, it may take you longer to grasp it fully. This can cause you to make some hefty mistakes if you are not careful.
- All in all, Ethereum should be analyzed and considered for investment, but the rewards need to be worth the risk.

Other Popular Cryptocurrencies

Besides Bitcoin and Ethereum, there are many other cryptocurrencies in the market. Here are five of the alternatives (Investopedia, 2021).

- **Litecoin**, known as the silver in comparison to Bitcoin's gold, was launched in 2011. It was designed by Charles Lee, formerly an engineer from Google. He created a cryptocurrency very similar to Bitcoin. One of its advantages is the faster speed at which the transactions are confirmed. Litecoin is known as the 6th largest cryptocurrency globally.
- **Polkadot,** known as DOT, shares a similarity to Ethereum, where a variety of blockchains can be connected or linked. Many people can use this

platform to design their own blockchains along with a certain element of guaranteed protection (something which is not offered in Ethereum). Designed by Gavin Wood, its market has capitalized up to $11.2 billion US since 2021.

- Another altcoin drawn from Bitcoin is **Bitcoin Cash** (BCH). It was one of the few successful changes made after debate by the larger public in regards to Bitcoin. (Considering its decentralized aspect, no one person can simply change and create an added crypto with Bitcoin.) The general problem was scalability. A blockchain has the ability to hold more data per block (8 MB) compared to the original 1 MB per block. This increases the transaction time, making it effective and efficient.

- **Stellar** (XLM) was designed with the intention of connecting large transactions with financial institutions through the use of blockchain. It is an open blockchain that can be used by the general public but has established itself in the entrepreneurial side for institutional transactions. It was created to remove the traditional intermediaries and hefty fees involved and was designed by Jed McCaleb.

- **Monero** (XMR) is an anonymous cryptocurrency launched in 2014 and uses a special technique known as 'ring signatures' (where a digital signature is created by a member that has their own personal key). Therefore, you can only make a transaction and sign it with your key. People will be able to see the transaction and the signature, but it will be impossible to determine who signed it. It is driven completely through donations and the community.

Cryptocurrency: The Roles It Can Play

The final, most daunting step is where you enter the live trading world. Don't discard paper trading entirely, as it is still good to practice or test new strategies in order to examine new results. Paper trading will save you a lot of money from potential mistakes and build an encouraging learning curve.

Now that you are familiar with cryptocurrency, it is also good to understand the different approaches you can take in regards to it. There are three common ways to earn money.

1. **Mining:** As we covered earlier, mining allows you to receive Bitcoins by participating in the verification of Bitcoin transactions.
2. **Investing:** is a long-term objective in growing one's income. Even in cryptocurrency, investors are in it for the long haul. Investors are not so fazed by the price fluctuations but rather focus on the future and the rewards.

3. **Trading:** is short-term, where people invest certain amounts of money, grow it, and leave when the value of the asset, stock, or currency reaches its peak. It requires a more hands-on approach and certainly entails that people will leave quickly if the market does not seem to have any more value. Traders have to gamble, determining when the market will crash and leaving in time to avoid a loss. It is certainly more of a game of analysis and strategy, and the most accurate traders tend to earn the most.

All in all, they are very similar to each other, but with different approaches. Investing and trading have goals to invest money in certain items to grow one's profit but over different periods of time. There are risks to both approaches, but trading is by far more heavily impacted by the nature of cryptocurrency, especially Bitcoin. With the endurance of investors, they could probably ride off the waves of deflated crypto prices and watch it rise again to a profitable level.

So should you consider simply using cryptocurrency as an investment or dealing it with it directly as a currency (whether to purchase or sell items online)?

Let's take a look at using cryptocurrency purely as currency and the pros and cons of using it for everyday purchases on the web. Whether you invest, trade, mine, or simply purchase, as long as you are aware of the risks and take extra care, then you are on a good path.

- If you want to remain more anonymous or remove third parties (to avoid excess fees) when making large transactions, then this is a viable option to undertake. Do keep in mind its volatile nature may backfire against you with any purchases made or received in that specific period of time.
- Not many countries actually accept cryptocurrency as a legal currency, thus limiting your options of what you can buy with it.
- Due to cryptocurrency's volatile nature, whatever you may be purchasing could spike in price, either up or down.
- Your transfer fees will be decreased, but you are also more likely to run into internet scams if you are not careful.

If you are looking for a safe form of investment, then cryptocurrency is not for you. Despite its promise of an enormously large reward, it could also lead to enormous losses. It is a little bit of a gamble, but Bitcoin has slowly but surely gained a higher and more popular foothold in this day and age. Many people are investing in cryptocurrency, specifically Bitcoin, because they hope it will grow huge in the future.

Either way, blockchain technology is here to stay, and it is best to understand how it runs and works in order to invest wisely.

Chapter 3: Understanding Public Blockchain

There are several different kinds of blockchains, for example, private, public, and federated. Each one is suited for a different platform and job, and each plays an important role in the web. In order to fully understand public blockchain, which was the first and original design, it must be compared to private blockchains.

Private blockchain is often used in large enterprises due to its ability to protect client's transactional information from hackers and data thieves. Therefore, despite the fact that it does not work on a decentralized platform, it builds security for any clients and businesses who decide to use it.

Public blockchains are open to the general public through the internet. Everyone can gain access to it, download it, and make transactions accordingly. It is truly a decentralized system and completely transparent. However, it is known to be slower and can attract the wrong kind of people considering anyone from anywhere who has an internet connection can gain access to it. But due to its ledger transparency and lack of third-party involvement, it is still viewed as more attractive considering there is no singular party who can control it.

Private blockchains are partially decentralized, but an individual or group of individuals have control over the programming and how it runs. Not everyone can have access to the ledgers either, and it is certainly not transparent. However, private blockchains do not have as many issues with malicious people or errors in the system. They are also much faster with transfers than public blockchains. The transfer fees are significantly less and should be considered for use in businesses and companies.

In order for private blockchains to work, those that have access to it need to be trusted, because of its general anonymous nature. It would be hard to see if anyone tampered with private blockchains. However, unlike public blockchains, private blockchains are regulated, controlled and work at significantly faster speeds. Private blockchains are also perfect for companies that value privacy, and can avoid leaks from data hackers or 'spies' online that could be detrimental to a business.

Where private and public blockchains are similar is that they synchronize data across different computers and allow the right level of security to make hacking difficult.

However, considering cryptocurrencies such as Bitcoin and Ethereum run on public blockchain, we'll take a more in-depth look at decentralized websites.

Decentralized Websites

Ever since the start of the internet, it has grown significantly. However, much to many people's dismay, platforms started being taken over by huge corporations who not only monitor and control freedom of speech but ultimately have control of most of the web. (Much like the banks, these corporations act as intermediaries deciding what information you see based on your online activity.) With a small number of companies having control over news and information, it is no wonder that there can be a level of corrupt influence and bias spread online. Whether for power, money, or keeping secrets hidden from the public, one can never truly tell how much has been silenced or edited.

Ever since the invention and design of Bitcoin, many people have used decentralized blockchain for other projects to resolve (or better yet remove) the control of large companies, placing it in the hands of the general public. As someone working in cryptocurrency and on decentralized platforms, it is wise to be aware of the growth of other decentralized websites. Being interested in having control of your money generally means you would appreciate having control of various other aspects on the web. Furthermore, the growth in popularity of decentralized websites may also boost the popularity of Bitcoin and other cryptocurrencies.

Decentralized websites work in a way that people can publish websites and content without a middleman involved. This adds to security, requires less constant monitoring, and lowers the number of privacy infringements from big corporations such Facebook, Instagram, and Twitter. It is seen as a way to take one's freedom back into their own hands and to allow greater freedom of speech.

However, there are a few projects underway, but nothing overtly official yet regarding decentralized websites. A few experimental programs are available such as Matrix (similar to WhatsApp), or OpenBazaar (a marketplace that has been decentralized).

Despite all the great implications of decentralized websites, there would also be some dark realities that will come with it.

- Although censorship is viewed in a negative light, it plays a positive role when it comes to controlling disturbing images, hate speech, cyberbullying, and more. It would be far more difficult to prevent these things on a platform that has no control, and unfortunately, there are many murky people working on the web.
- It also gets increasingly difficult to erase anything that may have been posted online, which could have major harmful impacts on people (depending on the post).
- Criminals will have more freedom online than ever before, for example, sending disturbing pictures that are encrypted. It is a dark reality of

privacy online as it opens many more doors for the wrong people to use and abuse.

All of these things need to seriously be taken into consideration before welcoming decentralized websites with open arms. The idea behind them is to run on Bitcoin's cryptic technology (public blockchain). However, considering both the pros and cons of Bitcoin, it is no wonder that decentralized websites may well be volatile and unpredictable. They will be less vulnerable to hackers but cannot prevent the wrong people from using the technology for hate, crime, and more. In the long run, public blockchain is an ingenious invention, but much like anything else, it is not perfect.

These are all things you need to know and take into consideration as you plan to invest in cryptocurrency. The web is constantly changing, but it is currently not known whether decentralized websites are the path to take or whether cryptocurrencies will become a globally united form of payment.

Chapter 4: Rules of Cryptocurrencies

A person may imagine that chaos may reign supreme with public blockchain and cryptocurrencies to which everyone can gain access. This is not the case, however, as even cryptocurrencies have rules and regulations people must follow. In order to have a certain element of order and stability, one must also have limitations. Cryptocurrencies are no exception to this.

In a world where more entrepreneurs are needed, cryptocurrencies give more control and power to those who are starting or running businesses. People can receive payments in a united currency, avoid heavy transfer fees, and be linked through a practically fraud-proof system.

Cryptocurrency Regulations

Many governments are against cryptocurrency due to lack of control, while others see the benefit of a huge economic boost. Opinions and points of view differ, and one must be aware of what exactly the rules are for the country that you live in. A person might tend to wonder why cryptocurrency is so heavily discouraged in some countries, yet highly encouraged in others. Some areas certainly have a different point of view regarding this, and it is best to understand why.

- At the rapid rate of popularity in which cryptocurrency is growing, it is no wonder that it can be seen as a potential boost to the economy. With many becoming rich literally overnight and others using it to generate income, cryptocurrency has amazing potential in the future.
- With slow or terrible service from banks in third-world countries, many may see this as a huge benefit and a step away from the centralized financial system. There are countless people who do not have access to banking services and have a greater chance of getting access to the internet, which in turn gives them access to cryptocurrency.
- Cryptocurrency takes away the control of greedy or corrupt regulators and places the assets directly into the owners' hands.

Countries Where Cryptocurrency Is Legal

There are many other countries that are partially against cryptocurrency or have implemented laws to regulate its use. In most of America, most of Europe, and some of Asia, cryptocurrency is legal and safe. The most developed countries typically allow cryptocurrency.

Country	Regulation
Canada	<ul><li>It is perfectly legal to use Bitcoin, whether to buy stock online or trade.</li><li>It is not accepted as an official form of currency.</li><li>Tax law applies to any transactions made digitally. Any profits or losses earned from cryptocurrency are liable for taxes and should be included in the income of the seller.</li><li>You must register with the Financial Transactions and Reports Analysis Centre of Canada (FINTRAC).</li></ul>

Columbia	• Columbia doesn't consider cryptocurrency as an official currency; therefore, it cannot be used against debts or in assessing one's net worth. • However, it is still legal to trade and invest but be aware of the risks.
Mexico	• Cryptocurrency is legal in Mexico. • Any digital transactions need to be reported, much like traditional currencies. • It is also viewed as an online transferable and legal asset known as a virtual asset (Regulation of Cryptocurrency Around the World, 2014) which means the bank can practice a certain element of control of major cryptocurrency investments, purchases, and sales.

United States	• The United States doesn't see cryptocurrency as illegal itself, but it does not view it as an official legal currency.
	• The regulations are different from state to state, and you may find it difficult to find all the legalities in regards to cryptocurrency.
	• There is tax guidance placed on cryptocurrency as it is seen as an asset in the eyes of the US government's Internal Revenue Service (IRS).
	• It is best to take careful notes and do your research in the state you live in to ensure you understand the rules.
Singapore	• It is legal to invest and work with cryptocurrency, but it is not seen as an official form of currency in this country either.
	• You will need to register with the Monetary Authority of Singapore.
	• Cryptocurrency is also viewed as assets by those in control of taxes and should be declared accordingly.

Japan	<ul><li>Cryptocurrency is seen both as a legal form of currency and an asset.</li><li>As of 2017, cryptocurrency is recognized as property.</li><li>Japan has had one of the most positive responses towards cryptocurrency and allows it to be regulated as a legal currency.</li></ul>
Australia	<ul><li>It is perfectly legal to use cryptocurrency in this country; however, it is not perceived as authentic money.</li><li>There have been no major interventions or regulations in Australia regarding the use of trading and selling cryptocurrency, making it easier to invest in without getting entangled in any legal issues.</li></ul>

Hong Kong	<ul><li>Hong Kong businesses adopted cryptocurrency at such a rapid speed that it caught the government's attention.</li><li>As of 2021, there are no immediate regulations made towards cryptocurrency, but that is not likely to remain so in the future.</li><li>It is best to keep an eye out for regulations and new rules in Hong Kong due to the ever-growing popularity of cryptocurrency among businesses.</li><li>It does not accept cryptocurrency as legal tender like Japan, but many businesses make use of it in investments all the same.</li></ul>

Italy	• Italy allows the use of buying, selling, and trading cryptocurrency as they themselves are proactive in becoming a cashless country. Thus, cryptocurrency may become exceedingly more popular. • Cryptocurrency legislation that was put in place mentions that anti-money laundering regulations are applicable to the providers of e-wallets and cryptocurrency exchanges.
United Kingdom	• There is no direct ban against cryptocurrency in the United Kingdom. • Warnings are given out about the dangers of investing in the online virtual market, but there are a few regulations in place. • One should check whether your cryptocurrency happens to land under Financial Services and Markets Act 2000's Electronic Money Regulations before thinking you are completely free of any rules.

Ireland	• Ireland has also issued related warnings of cryptocurrency risks, but there is no direct ban or local regulations that have currently been implemented.

Crypto Bans

In some countries, cryptocurrency has been banned for multiple reasons that you should be aware of. Whether you are residing or merely visiting a certain country, it is best to stay on the right side of the law.

Cryptocurrency is banned in certain countries because:
- Governments have absolutely no control or regulation over this form of currency. Because of this lack of control, they may deem this type of currency as a threat to power or loss of tax income.
- Since users are generally anonymous and have full control while sending transactions, it is easier for suspicious transactions to take place from time to time.
- When large investments are placed into cryptocurrency, there is a massive risk involved, and, therefore, it is discouraged due to the negative impact it can have on the economy.

- It threatens the banks, institutions, and businesses, as cryptocurrency removes the middleman (the role which banks normally play).

Some of the top countries that ban cryptocurrency at the moment are:

Country	Regulation
Algeria	- There is a full ban; using cryptocurrency is 100% illegal with no exception.
Bolivia	- There is a full ban; the government wants control and regulation over currency and to protect the people from Ponzi schemes, etc.
North Macedonia	- Cryptocurrency is 100% illegal, and this is the only country in Europe that is so against cryptocurrency.
Morocco	- You can face jail time for using cryptocurrency in this country, showing the severity of how much the country is against this form of digital currency.

Initial Coin Offering

Another term you may come across in the cryptocurrency world is initial coin offering (ICO). In the simplest terms, it is a fundraiser program to raise money to launch new versions of cryptocurrency, very similar to an initial public offering when a company goes public on the stock market.

Designers will host a campaign with a project plan and map of their goals in order to encourage investors to add a contribution and get a return in coin once it has been launched. It is highly risky, but there have been many successful ICO ventures, such as Mastercoin, Ethereum, and Waves. It is good for an investor who is low on funding to consider.

There are very few, if any, government regulations with the ICO process, and though it is a gold mine of potential, it is also a hotspot for scammers. If you want to consider investing in an ICO, here are some steps you need to keep yourself safe. If anything smells like a scam or con to you, then it probably is.

- Like anything else that you want to spend your money on, do your research first. Find out the ICO plans and assess for yourself whether the risk is worth the reward.
- Check and see whether their project involves blockchain. If neither of these is required in the

investment, then you are looking at a probable scammer.

- If empty or non-existent GitHubs (platforms that host coding) are proposed, this is also likely to be a scam.
- It's all in the details. If the proposed project lacks detail, then it is best to stay far away from it.
- When the project plays favoritism with the development team, you are looking at another probable scam—the development team will receive the most funds or returns on investment.
- Teams are often named; therefore, if you do your research, you may come to realize a project may be using a group of non-professionals or beginners or have no full-time developers in their employ. Whether through Google or databases such as LinkedIn or other social media, if the information on their bio does not match or doesn't appear anywhere else online, then this is another warning sign.
- A project with unclear goals is also another surefire way to root out a scam.

All in all, ICO is risky, and people should be wise regarding the decisions they make.

Other Cryptocurrency Scams

One of the worst possible ways to lose your money and investments are through scams, yet this is a common occurrence. People are flooded with scam emails, messages, and website links every single day. Therefore, it is no surprise that there are scams littered throughout cryptocurrency investments. Here are some of the top scams to look out for and steps to ensure you stay safe and smart while investing.

E-Wallets

Possibly the most direct and easiest route to steal one's money is through a person's e-wallet. This is a high target area for hackers and scammers. In June 2020, there was a massive hack in which several thousand email addresses and personal details were stolen. This also happened to Poloniex (a crypto asset exchange) near the end of 2019 (Osborne, 2020).

Here are the best ways to protect yourself :

- Avoid the use of public Wi-Fi, especially when accessing your accounts. Public Wi-Fi, although convenient, opens up easy network doors for hackers to break in and steal information, including your e-wallet if you log in. As tempted as you may be at the convenience, it is just not safe.
- Ensure each and every file you download onto your computer, laptop, tablet, or even smartphone is safe. Hackers love attaching malware to files and folders, which can creep in and steal your info. Do take note—most hackers

cannot directly access your computer without you reciprocating it on your side. Whether it is through a website link, file, or email, consider this as a thief who needs you to unlock the door first before they can enter. However, they are a master of disguises. This is why you need to be extra careful.

- Use two-factor authentication (two methods of verifying your identity, typically through a password and a code that is sent to a cell phone number). Without your phone at hand, hackers will be unable to access your accounts. Two-factor authentication works as double security and makes your account so much stronger against cyberattacks.

- Saving your private keys in an offline database such as an external hard drive will limit the amount a thief can take. This is like a thief (hacker) gaining access to your house but with limited tools. They cannot access your safe (offline storage) in which you keep your valuables. This can buy you time to respond to a data breach.

Fake Websites

This is a common scam and not just specifically with cryptocurrency. However, it is quite common where people build websites almost identical to the legitimate cryptocurrency pages themselves (such as Ethereum's official page). It steals any data you may input and can potentially implant malware simply by accessing your computer.

To avoid this:

- Check the website you are typing in, especially if you were referred to it by a friend. Malware and fake sites sometimes only have the slightest difference in them, perhaps even having just one letter or digit changed.
- There are websites designed to scan and ensure the link you are visiting is safe. For example, on Trend Micro's website, you can enter a website link and see whether or not it has a virus attached.
- A professional website will almost never have a misspelling. However, many scam websites will, either due to sloppiness or because the correctly spelled URL is already taken by the authentic company.
- Secure website URLs start with "https" instead of "http." The 's' can make all the difference in the world when spotting scammers. Not all "http" sites are scams; however, in regards to cryptocurrency, you can be ensured that legitimate sites will be secure.

If you were to look at these two websites, which one is likely to be the scam?

1. http://etheream.org/en/

2. https://ethereum.org/en/

The answer would be the first one, where it begins with "http" (meaning it is not secure), and there is a misspelling. However, at a quick glance, no one would really be able to tell the difference.

But when you are working with money online, you have to be careful. Double-check and triple-check new sites as you can never be too careful when it comes to your money

Mobile App Scammers

Much like fake websites, fake mobile apps are bound to occur too. They can easily upload scams on app stores, and although they tend to get removed quickly, the damage can be done.

- Again, check for misspellings, compare the logo, and even use tutorials on YouTube to compare to the one you want to download.
- A general rule of thumb is also to check the reviews. Do not download any app if it has no reviews, especially cryptocurrency ones. People get verbal online when something is a scam, and you are bound to find many complaints left by means of comments on the fake app.

Be Extra Cautious of Social Media Ads

Ads on social media platforms can also be practically run by anybody. Therefore, fake news, links, and websites can be sent to you, and there is a danger if you immediately fall for it and click a link.

- As a general rule of thumb, check any hyperlink on social media with Trend Micro or any other anti-virus apps before accessing the links.
- Check the comments (if there are any) to see other people's responses. It is unlikely that you were the first to see the ad.
- Instead of going through social media links regarding cryptocurrency, rather go through the official website link and find what you need from there.
- Beware of news posts from celebrities promoting crypto sites; don't use their endorsement as a form of safeguard. Fake news happens almost as easily as rain, and one has to triple-check everything one sees on social media.

Con Emails

Just like any form of communication, email is a floodgate for spammers, and one should be careful what they click and read.

- Take note that scammers on email can send relatively authentic-looking emails; however, they add subtle signs of urgency within the message to cause you to click without thinking. For example, these could be threats of accounts being shut down within a matter of hours or asking you for urgent information updates.
- Don't click on links provided via email. Again, this is like opening a doorway for a hacker to enter your computer. Rather access your account through the official method to see if any of the claims on email are true.
- Scan the links, or check out the URL. You can do so by slightly hovering your mouse over where you should click the link. But do not actually click on the link! If you want to copy and scan a link, remember to right-click and copy the link address (if you are working on a computer or laptop that is).
- Accidental clicking on links is also possible. If this occurs on your computer or laptop, click CTRL + W on a PC as quickly as possible to sever the connection before anything happens.

Cheaper Is Not Always Better

The temptation to purchase cheaper coins is always there, but remember, when an offer is too good to be true, then it normally is. Research the cryptocurrency you want to invest in and make 100% sure it is legitimate. Bitcoin and Ethereum have been around long enough to be able to verify their authenticity. However, many other forms of smaller cryptocurrency have sprung up around the globe. It can be truly hard at times to determine what is real and what is not. Thorough research can weed most scammers out. If you are not entirely sure the cryptocurrency is a scam or legitimate, then stay far away.

Bitcoin Mining Scams

Keep an eye on guaranteed promises. As bad as this sounds, no legitimate investor company can promise you an absolute guaranteed return. Many scammers try to hook unsuspecting people with the allure of big rewards, not mentioning the hundreds of fees they tag along with the returns.

Scammer Money Requests

Sometimes people hack others' social media accounts and can afford to be blasé enough to ask people for money via cryptocurrency, especially if it is a celebrity. Be very cautious of this, even if it comes from a friend. Always double-check (like calling your friend or family member) and remember that the person behind the screen is not always who you think they are. Scammers have lying and deceiving down to an art form, but the easiest way to prevent this is double-checking and doing your research.

Ponzi Schemes

When you enter the crypto investment world, you will almost be guaranteed to hear about Ponzi schemes and how devastating they can be to a business. Hopefully, you will never fall for a scheme like this yourself, so it is best to familiarize yourself in order to learn how to avoid it.

So what exactly is a Ponzi scheme?

A Ponzi scheme occurs when one pays prior investors with money they have received from new investors while also keeping some money for themselves. Unlike most investment scams that carry on for a short while before disappearing, Ponzi schemes can last for years or even up to a decade. With anonymity online, it takes much longer to root out fraudsters than with regulated currencies.

In order for these Ponzi schemes to continue, they need money from constant new members to pay out the older investors. People think they are getting a profit; however, they are losing money at a rapid pace.

Ponzi scheme initiators try to convince not only you but also your family and friends to get involved. The idea behind the scheme is to gain as many investors as possible.

Unfortunately, Ponzi schemes are quite common in the world of cryptocurrency. It is best to watch for the following signs in order to avoid falling for one:

- Ponzi schemes tend to claim their investments have little to no risk with a high-profit return. However, especially with cryptocurrency, this is too good to be true.
- Habitual returns (returns that are made on a consistent basis in a volatile market) are, ironically enough, a sign of a scammer. There is no way to predict or have a consistent return. With cryptocurrencies, you will have ups and downs.
- Pay attention to investments that are not regulated by the US Securities and Exchange Commission (SEC) or others. It is best always to check and double-check whether the investments are regulated or not.

- If someone with whom you have no prior history contacts you asking you to invest, this is usually a sign of a scam. Basically, scammers can target you by tracking your cell or email and contacting you out of the blue. You may have inadvertently provided your contact information by entering it on a website or signing up for a subscription. The scammer may also have paid third-party businesses to gain your contact information.
- There is a sense of urgency. Scammers want to trick you into investing before you have the proper time to think or do your research. Never rush into something, especially if it is online, and don't ever let anyone talk you into making an immediate payment. You will save yourself a lot of money (even from legitimate salespeople who con you into buying more than you should). Take a step back—if you see them pushing hard, this is an immediate red flag.

Pyramid Schemes

You have likely heard of the term pyramid scheme, yet in all honesty, you might not understand what it is exactly. Considering this is another scheme to watch out for in the crypto world, it is best to understand it to help you to avoid it.

A pyramid scheme is an active recruiter scheme where people pay to be a part of a membership of some kind.

A portion of their membership payment tends to go to people who have been recruited as members before them (as a commission). The new members then actively work on recruiting others in order to gain more income. So the pyramid gradually grows where prior members receive the income from new recruits until eventually the trough dries out, and no more people are recruited. Some of the more established members might leave with loads of cash in their pockets, while others are simply caught empty-handed. The pyramid scheme is illegal in many countries, but not all. However, it is a good thing to look out for and be aware of.

Multi-level marketing is a type of pyramid scheme that is typically used by perfectly legal businesses that use a combination of income, such as sales of products or services combined with membership user fees. However, it isn't mandatory for the people involved to keep recruiting others, unlike other pyramid schemes.

Pyramid schemes may seem similar to Ponzi schemes; however, Ponzi schemes are illegal, less stealthy, do not use any products or forms of businesses to operate, and are more likely to scam you out of all your money.

OneCoin is a good example of a cryptocurrency pyramid scheme and a Ponzi scheme. Founded in 2014, instead of recruiting members or selling products, one was enticed to purchase OneCoin. Those who purchased it also promoted it, claiming that OneCoin would be Bitcoin's successor. It grew in popularity and traction, and many people purchased membership in return for OneCoin and the ability to mine for more.

However, one could only sell an amount that was strictly limited, and there were many red flags. Through their extreme and charming marketing tactics, the scheme initiators were able to catch many unsuspecting investors. However, there were many others that could see straight through the scam.

The OneCoin scam fell apart in 2016 after all the lies and empty promises, and an investigation was made in order to ascertain exactly what was taking place. New accounts were opened and the fraudulent activities were revealed. There have been an estimated 10,000 OneCoin victims and many more coming to light, leaving many in trauma and with a huge loss of income (Bartlett, 2020).

Pump-and-Dump

Pump-and-dump builds on the fear of investors missing out, but how do they do this? They "seek to artificially inflate the price of an asset through coordinated bulk buying and overly-hyped promotion through false advertising" (Declan Igoe, 2020). Then, in the end, they sell their assets, which allows the value to sink suddenly, as fast as it arose. In simplified terms, people use media together with a cash investment. They start purchasing large amounts of cryptocurrency at a rapid pace. This pushes the value higher. At the same time, the initiators promote the hype related to their targeted cryptocurrency's sudden growth spurt. Investors who see this opportunity dive in to take part, boosting the growth and value of the cryptocurrency. However, those who initiated the pump-and-dump sell their shares, making a major profit then exiting, allowing the cryptocurrency to plummet in its value and leaving investors at a loss.

Stories of Other Bitcoin Scams

Anne Sraders identified several other Bitcoin scams, of which we'll quickly mention a few (The Street Investing, 2020).

- Fake Bitcoin exchange, BitKRX, posed as an affiliate branch, resembling a respectable organization in South Korea. The designers used the resemblance of the trusted organization Korean Exchange (KRX) and scammed multiple people out of their money. BitKRX was exposed, however, in 2017.
- MiningMax was a nightmare Ponzi Bitcoin scam. The site was not registered with the US Securities and Exchange Commission, and it worked on the same basic strategy of Ponzi schemes. People placed a $3,200 US investment

into the business and received a total of $200 whenever they managed to refer someone to the company.

- My Big Coin was plainly and squarely a fake Bitcoin scam. Simply put, it was a replica, and it managed to fool a lot of people, stealing over $6 million US dollars in total. They were sued, however, and exposed.
- Mybtgwallet.com managed to lure unsuspecting investors into over $3.2 million US with the supposed promises of Bitcoin gold.

What to Do if You Have Been Scammed

Remember to follow the principle of not investing what you cannot afford to lose. This way, if you do get caught in a scam, it won't leave you bankrupt or in huge financial trouble. Here are some other steps you can take to minimize the loss when you have been scammed:

- Save others the same harm by reporting the scam and adding as much detail as possible. This will not just save countless other smart investors from falling into the same pit, but hopefully, it will expose the scammers as such to get them to shut down. Contact the Fraudulent Crypto Investment Platform (in the US) or the relevant financial authorities in your specific country. Provide in-depth detail and hope that most of your money gets recovered. Before investing, it is also best to do proactive research and find out who you should contact if you get caught in a scam.

- Be loud and be social. Spread the news about the scam as far as possible. This will place a dent in their scheme, and seeking help online may get you the answers you need to recover your money.
- Be sure to alert the people who developed your e-wallet app that the payments you made were to a scammer. This will allow them to build precautions and warn others who try to make payments to the same scammers.
- There are Bitcoin recovery services available where you can hire experts to use their technical expertise to track and recover as much money as possible for you. You should consider this option when you have lost large amounts.

In the end, it is very hard to recover the money that has been stolen from fraud. Even if you report it to the police (which you should), people who commit these crimes are very hard to catch. Considering that cryptocurrency's very reputation is built on anonymity and security, it does not allow much room for evidence. It is not completely impossible, but do not get your hopes up too high. This should not completely discourage you from investing in cryptocurrency. Rather this knowledge should act as a guide to keep you safe from the dangers that these forms of investments pose. Scammers are everywhere online, extending beyond cryptocurrency, so no matter where you are or what you do, play smart and never jump into anything without doing your own research.

Chapter 5: Mistakes Beginners Make

If you are on social media, I bet you have seen some bizarre posts or 'life hacks' that people try to promote as real. Social media is not a reliable source. So it is not surprising that people who tend to listen to the advice of others regarding cryptocurrency on these social media platforms could easily crash and burn on false rumors, wrong ideas, and news that spreads like wildfire. Yet this is one of the top mistakes that beginners in cryptocurrency tend to make.

As a beginner in any form or practice, one is bound to make mistakes, but you can learn from them. However, some errors can be costly. Scams and fraud are not the only ways you can lose money on this platform,

Let's now cover eight common beginner mistakes and how you can avoid them.

Top Eight Beginner Mistakes

Believing that you will quickly master trading and investing is setting yourself up to fail and quit when you do make a mistake. Don't set unrealistic expectations of the market, and especially, don't set unrealistic expectations for yourself. Learn from the mistakes of others!

Mistake Number 1

First off, ensure you are familiar with cryptocurrency terms as we cover in this book. A lack of knowledge in terminology or making assumptions about definitions is a quick mistake anyone can make. Here's a brief recap of some terms we've already mentioned and a few others that you may encounter.

- ICO: Initial Coin Offering

- Node: Laptops or PCs or any computer that can connect to a blockchain

- Altcoin: any coins that were designed and copied after Bitcoin

- FUD: Fear, uncertainty, and doubt

- Satoshi: small part or fraction of a Bitcoin

Mistake Number 2

Emotion is a powerful weapon, and people love to use it against you. Whether through peer pressure, fear, or excitement, you cannot afford to have your emotions get the better of you. Many scammers catch people this way, and uninformed decisions are the worst thing you can do when entrusting your money to someone.

Patience is key to not getting caught up in the rush of social media news and groups; they often share false or inaccurate news that prompts you to make an impulsive action. Often social media is ripe with phishing scams and troublemakers who love to stir things up with a simple message. So be patient and take your time to verify the facts that you read about online.

The social media platform Twitter is very guilty of sharing false rumors and news. Do not trust everything that you read on this app, and double-check everything before investing.

Don't deviate from your trading plan out of panic or fear of missing out; rather, stick to your guns. In trading or investing, there will be losses, and there will be gains, but if you jump ahead or panic and change your strategy, you will find yourself receiving the short-end of the stick when it comes to trading. If you have developed a strong and solid strategy, stick to it until definitive proof comes along that you need to change.

Don't get caught up in believing in the common misconceptions that get spread around cryptocurrency. Get-rich-quick schemes are rife, and despite there being a small limited number of actual people who scored, much like those who win the lottery, the odds of it happening to you are too small for you to risk your entire financial well-being. There are many who take out loans, withdraw their pension or find other forms of money to invest in hopes of becoming the next billionaire. However, time and again, people have ended up ruining their financial well-being because of this. Play your cards well and wisely, and don't involve any unnecessary risk. You will thank yourself in the long term.

Pay particular attention to revenge trading that gets triggered by emotion. This occurs when you may have just incurred a loss, and you jump into an even riskier trade in order to cut your losses. However, anything done on impulse or emotion may cost you far more than your initial loss. Learning to take the loss and move on is always your best step forward. When you're new at trading, you will react hard to losses, but you can learn to react wisely from the beginning and save yourself even more regret. Most traders (even the pros) have losses, but their wise and tactful decisions build up their success later on.

Mistake Number 3

Without a strategy, you will very likely end up losing money. You need to have clear targets and goals, and although it can be good to regularly adjust those strategies, you may find that sticking to your guns will pay off in the long run. Endurance is hard to practice but worth every penny when it comes to investing.

Having no clear strategy or goals for your cryptocurrency investments is like walking into a forest with no map or compass. You will get lost, and you are likely to lose a lot of assets along the way. Strategy walks alongside research, and therefore, in order to form a powerful strategy, you need to do the research. Scammers love people who have no true strategy or thorough knowledge, preying on their ignorance and quick decision-making that comes with this mistake.

For example, those who sold Bitcoin when it jumped from $100 to $3,000 sorely regretted it after it reached a peak of $20,000, as did the person who spent 10,000 Bitcoins for pizza. Today, those Bitcoins would literally be worth thousands more.

Furthermore, having a strategy avoids the craze of panic and allows reason and logic to set in during the tough times. With cryptocurrency, it is easy to panic when a currency deflates over one hour; yet, it may jump three times higher several hours later, but you already sold your shares and are left with an immense loss of profit. This can cost you potentially hundreds if not thousands of dollars in a panicked moment.

Mistake Number 4

Not using stop-loss orders is a huge mistake a beginner can make. So what is a stop-loss order? As an example, if your investment is doing well, but you are wary that a dip in the market may occur, you can set a stop-loss order at a 5% decline. If the cryptocurrency does decline more than 5%, your assets will automatically be pulled out and traded into US dollars, saving you time and financial loss.

You can also set stop-loss orders on your entire cryptocurrency portfolio. According to Cryptocurrency Portfolio Stop-Loss (2020), "portfolio stop-losses pull the entire portfolio out of the market when a stop-loss is triggered."

This is useful to cut as many losses in trading as possible. Not using this can cost you all your assets if you are not careful, and most wise traders make use of this.

Mistake Number 5

Instead of seeing profits or losses in terms of actual dollars, the best way to view them is by using percentages. Get into the habit of comparing as such, which allows the mindset of cryptocurrency to flow better.

Mistake Number 6

Be sure that you don't enter the market at its all-time high. What goes up must eventually go down, right? And if you invest when it is at the top, it will only set you up for a downhill slope, and there is no guarantee of recovery.

Mistake Number 7

Don't fall for the latest and newest altcoin that is claimed to replace or overtake Bitcoin. Bitcoin has been dominating the market and will likely for years to come. People who say otherwise use fear of missing out and manipulation techniques in order to get people to invest. There will always be new cryptocurrencies that arise, but most of them will not survive in the long haul.

Mistake Number 8

Although good analysis and keeping track of your coin prices are good habits, doing so too often each day will put unmerited stress on your emotions. Save yourself the stress and learn to take a break. Despite the volatile nature of cryptocurrency, it is not likely to pour your finances down the drain if you miss an update between minutes or even hours.

All in all, be careful when handling your investment online. It is a tricky world, and the best thing you can do for yourself is to be prepared.

Chapter 6: Looking to the Future

When looking back at the overall history of cryptocurrency, one might wonder what lies on the road ahead. There are many speculations. Some people have high hopes, and others believe that failure lies in cryptocurrencies' course. However, the best you can take is to look at the facts and decide for yourself what road you think cryptocurrency might just take.

One thing you should take into consideration is the future of security online, especially regarding online transactions.

Tokenization

Since its creation in 2001, tokenization has slowly but surely been gaining in popularity. Tokenization encrypts data into a series of algorithmic numbers, which is called a token. This is meant to protect sensitive data such as credit card details in the process of making payments. For example, when someone makes a payment online via tokenization, the customer's account number will be substituted with various random numbers that are automatically created. The system will then proceed with the payment through the bank while keeping all data secure. Tokens work as a placeholder, which is far safer than having one's actual account number details exposed on the web. However, any data that is viewed as valuable can be tokenized, not just financial data.

The ultimate goal of tokenization, much like blockchain, is to prevent tampering from hackers. It's a heavy form of cybersecurity meant to protect your data online.

Encryption

Over the years, many people have claimed to love the security that encryption holds. Encryption transforms sensitive data in some form or code, and the only way to decipher and read it is to have access to the decryption key to read it. Much like tokenization, its intent is to protect people's sensitive data from online scammers and hackers.

Despite being a secure form of handling data, more people have come to accept and switch over to tokenization rather than encryption. One is only left to wonder which form of cybersecurity is better, especially in the future.

To fully comprehend and understand the two security systems, it is best to assess their respective strengths and weaknesses to see who will prevail.

Pros and Cons of Tokenization

Pros:
- The data that hackers look for in the businesses themselves are no longer available to them due to tokenization, thus relieving many businesses of the enormous pressure of always having to keep client's data safe from hackers.
- It is good for small businesses that are especially vulnerable to hackers.
- Unlike encryption, the data itself is sent as a series of algorithmic numbers, making it useless to a hacker if intercepted.

Cons:
- Tokenization systems have become a target for people who scam or create fraud themselves, whether by creating look-alike pages or literally becoming tokenization programs themselves.
- It would be more difficult to implement such a system in a mass-scale business; therefore, it might just be easier to create or hire a decent encryption expert.
- There is a considerable cost when it comes to implementing tokens in your business. A

business would have to decide whether they can afford it and if the extra security is indeed worth the price.

Pros and Cons of Encryption

Pros:

- Encryption is easy and not complicated to set up.
- It can work on a large scale basis for any business.
- The encryption runs through all the data, including backups, which hackers may have seen as vulnerable points to exploit.

Cons:

- Encryption cannot protect you from inside attacks. Anyone who has access to a decipher key has access to the crucial data. This is especially concerning if you have a large number of people who have access.
- Hackers have been able to breach through encryption, so it isn't hacker-proof.

Both have their pros and cons, and both are still planned to be used in the future. However, tokenization and cryptocurrency are starting to become connected, which should be taken into consideration when looking to the future.

Tokenized Assets

In 2016, an idea surfaced to combine tokenization and cryptocurrency by learning how to transfer real digital assets via blockchain through tokens. The idea was to take Bitcoin's advantages and combine them securely with legal assets. These are known as tokenized assets.

The advantages of tokenized assets are:

- The liquidity of one's assets would amplify with this form of financial transfers. Items that need high security can be sold due to the discreet and encrypted ways of both blockchain and tokenization combined.
- Doors for more investments would open due to the fact that, worldwide, more people have access to internet connection than proper banking services. This could potentially boost the economy and the growth of businesses as well as benefiting the general public.
- The tokens would be vastly cheaper as well and easily lowering the minimum rate of investment, furthermore increasing stock liquidity.
- Customers' and investors' biggest issues in regards to business is a lack of transparency and truth in regards to the expenditures and overall finances decisions a business makes, yet the use of public blockchain allows a better peek into

the finances of the business through its public ledgers. The information will be available 24/7, building foundational trust with their investors.

The disadvantages of tokenized assets include:

- Although the idea is there, launching programs such as these at such a huge scale is a challenge in and of itself.
- The ability to determine legal jurisdiction in different countries will make things infinitely harder.
- Enforcing the security of tokens is much more difficult via blockchain and poses a great challenge for the time being.
- The doorway to scams and hacking are slightly wider as more people have access to investing.
- The economies have been very wary of blockchain in general and may take a while to accept this form of financial transfers.
- Although the transfer and its general info will be encrypted and secure, the keys and e-wallets are still vulnerable to hacks and theft.

China's Plan for Cryptocurrency

China has always had a complicated but important relationship with cryptocurrency. There was a point in time during Bitcoin's growth that China had the lead in Bitcoin miners and had a massive exchange volume.

History of China and Bitcoin

In 2007, Tencent in China, providers of internet and phone services, created and launched Q Coin, which intended for these coins as a reward that could be used for some of its services. However, unwittingly, the Q Coin turned into a secondary market, and the government effectively shut it down. There were, however, 221 million people who were Tencent's services at the time, and they had become familiar with virtual currency (CrytpoVantage, 2020).

By 2009, the government also shut down another secondary market where the trade of real goods for virtual currency had been created for wealthy gamers who wanted others to do the work for them in order to get a boost in their games.

Therefore, unlike the rest of the world, people in China had an active knowledge of virtual currency, thus playing a heavy role in Bitcoin.

In 2010-2014, there were no massive or strict regulations placed in China in regards to Bitcoin. This allowed room for creativity and the traction of Bitcoin to grow amongst the people in China.

In 2011, the Chinese Bitcoin Exchange (BTCC) was created, but in 2013 it gained a popular boost from the people in China. Much like any other country, Bitcoin had only been receiving a bad rap in its early years. In April 2013, China's One Foundation allowed and accepted donations using Bitcoin to raise funds after an earthquake had struck the country. The large value of donations received allowed people to view Bitcoin in a far more positive light than before. In May, a crypto exchange by the name of Huobi was also launched, meant intentionally for Bitcoin mining.

"BTTChina became the largest crypto exchange in the world by volume, surpassing the now-infamous Mt. Gox" (CryptoVantage, 2020). Bitcoin value reached an 800% increase, causing a spike and instigating a global adoption of this currency. However, in 2013, December, Baidu (the Chinese state search engine) and Taobao (an e-commerce site) were forced to remove the option of buying and selling with Bitcoin, as it was no longer a legal tender. Many banks and the ministries of government had created a statement to do so.

However, despite the fact that one could not directly use it in the country, it was still very much legal to mine and trade with it. Many types of affordable hardware were created in order to mine Bitcoins in China, allowing and encouraging its constant and renewed growth in the country. By August 2015, half of the network of Bitcoin miners came from China.

In September 2017, China's government banned initial coin offerings due to the high growth rate and the extreme risk that was involved. Currencies that weren't considered legal tender and backed by the government (called non-fiat fees) were then discouraged as many simply stopped using them. The government put a ban on exchanging cryptocurrencies to fiat (legal currency that is backed by the government). Bitcoin and other cryptocurrencies were rendered as having no value in China.

In 2018, the government set up its Great Firewall on the web and banned exchanges of crypto. Yet, despite all this work into rooting out cryptocurrency, China certainly had a vast and extensive interest in blockchain technology. Chinese President Xi Jinping himself declared that any important advancement in technology would involve blockchain. China would find ways to support this technology and help grow and advance it in their country.

China's New Cryptocurrency

Digital Currency/Electronic Payments (DCEP) was founded and designed by the Chinese state. A digitized version of yuan, the Chinese official currency, China has hopes for it to advance and become a global currency for people to use worldwide.

The underlying reason for the success of DCEP is the large population (over 39 million) of Chinese people that live around the globe. However, there are still rising concerns over the intentions behind DCEP.

Using blockchain technology to host it, DCEP uses a digitalized ledger for each and every transaction that comes through. The difference is that DCEP is still largely in control of the government. This centralizes the currency, which is the exact opposite strategy of Bitcoin and other cryptocurrencies that focus on decentralization. This may remove some of its initial value.

However, at the time of this writing, DCEP is being used and tested out in certain cities in China by allowing people to use an e-wallet rather than banks. There is exceeding pressure to launch this cryptocurrency as soon as possible.

China wishes to internationalize DCEP to break a certain amount of control that America has with its virtual currency called Libra—which was announced in 2019 with the intention of having people sell and buy items with minimal fees. One would be able to transfer or 'cash out' Libra online or even at a grocery store. People would have to use a wallet called Calibra Wallet, also owned by Facebook, that will be designed into WhatsApp and Messenger alongside an app of its own. It stands in direct competition with China's DCEP.

It does appear that China's DCEP is winning, though. The reason is that Libra is designed under a large organization (Facebook) whereas the DCEP has the backing of the Chinese government. Libra is also struggling to gain the approval of the American government, which is slowing its progress down at a significant rate.

All in all, if the DCEP were to win, it would have a significant impact on Western currency, especially the power imposed through the American dollar. Whether it is a good or a bad thing is certainly unknown. But as someone who wants to or plans to invest in cryptocurrency, it would be wise to keep yourself updated on the growth of both Libra and the Chinese DCEP. The world is changing ever so rapidly, and it is best to take every opportunity that is knocking on the door.

There are hopes for China to become a cashless society, and it has come to the point where cryptocurrency might just be the next big thing.

Advantages of DCEP

- Multiple countries do not have the money to afford bank fees, yet the use of DCEP will be allowed with minimal fees. This will allow and target other third-world countries in desperate need of financial services alongside poorer communities in China.
- Government financial operations will be able to run more efficiently with the use of DCEP.

Disadvantages of DCEP

- Removal of cash transactions allows for less anonymity regarding payments. Many, if not most, of the citizens will then be tracked and potentially controlled over their financial choices.
- The bank's use or authority to also set negative interest rates could be cause for big concern. Negative interest rates are used to encourage spending and discourage people from saving, which could potentially weaken the currency.
- The financial system could potentially be destabilized with the use of DCEP, and many other programs and systems will have to be put in place to ensure this does not happen.

There is no sure way of telling how DCEP will work out in the future. More people will have access to financial services, yet it can come with the control of an iron fist from the government. Many of those who use Bitcoin are precisely aware of this and the dangers that could potentially come from the use of this cryptocurrency. Yet, the advantages of breaking some of the financial control America has over the virtual world may not necessarily be a bad thing either. One can only watch and wait but also be aware of China's role in global cryptocurrency in the near future. The uncertainty may be daunting, especially after a global pandemic and a recession that is spread across the globe. The best thing would be to watch and wait, and to do you research. it is best to see the facts and decide for yourself whether or not you would want to partake in these new oncoming global cryptocurrencies, or whether the risk is too high.

Chapter 7: Investing in Tech Companies

Nothing quite hypes up someone's belief in a modern and futuristic world than looking down on a city from a skyscraper to observe all the buildings below. The world has changed above and beyond, and investing is a serious matter to take into consideration when thinking ahead for yourself. One would believe that you should also invest in the future, so it is no surprise if technology companies are the first ones that come to mind. This is especially true if those companies take an interest in the various forms of cryptocurrency as well. It would be wise to find out a little more about them and see if they are similarly worth investing in (alongside cryptocurrencies). Tech companies like Tesla are working to allow people to purchase their products with Bitcoin.

Tech companies are rising up, especially in the midst of a global pandemic. The world of personal interaction was replaced, if for a temporary while, with digital communication. Amazon's stock and value surged, so many would come to believe the advantage of investing in a tech company.

Firstly, one should realize that tech companies rely on technology beyond smartphones, computers, televisions, or tablets. Technology companies also spend time creating and developing artificial intelligence (AI) such as chatbots, and they create and develop software, playing a role in practically all parts of the world today.

The best technology companies to look for are companies that sell and buy products using the web. Companies that create and design hardware such as smartphones (Apple and Android being the two common examples) are good to consider, as are software companies that create apps, programs, and even websites. It is especially good to consider those who have taken an interest in cryptocurrency or have been recommended to do so. Considering that both tech companies and cryptocurrencies are seen as innovations for the future, doesn't it make sense that they both should work together side by side?

Tech companies are growing by the day as there is ever-increasing demand especially in regards to software and coding. The digital world is expanding, and it is best to get the greatest benefit out of it by investing wisely. There are multiple opportunities that come with investing in tech stock, including the fact that it is new and trending and won't grow out of fashion any time soon.

Doing one's research well will allow you to find potential tech companies that have higher chances of growing and better opportunities to give you a return. There still is a certain element of risk involved where companies manufacture products that backfire. For example, when the Galaxy Note 7 was designed and launched, it ended up having multiple cases of exploding batteries. Not only did this cause a major financial loss, but it also gave a massive blow to the company's reputation. However, mistakes like these can so easily happen when you are entering a brand new world of technology.

Investing in tech is also a complicated area to understand, and therefore a lot of research and work needs to be done in order to fully grasp and strategize the steps you need to take in order to be successful with your investments. As a norm, technology is a complicated field, so it is no surprise that investing in it would be too. To determine whether an investment may prove fruitful, check out its history. However, many tech companies are new, so there is still an extreme level of unpredictability of how things may go. Much like cryptocurrency, it allows the market to be slightly volatile, which is a risk you need to take into consideration.

So you have decided that you do want to invest in tech companies, but where do you start? Here are some of the top tech companies that you can consider investing in.

Looking at Tesla

Tesla is an American company that dedicates itself to producing electric cars and sustainable energy. It sounds like something out of a science fiction movie. They believe in developing methods to draw people away from fossil fuels and to thrust them into the future of clean electricity. This is very necessary for this day and age, where pollution and waste run rampant.

"Launched in 2008, the Roadster unveiled Tesla's cutting-edge battery technology and electric powertrain. From there, Tesla designed the world's first-ever premium all-electric sedan from the ground up—Model S—which has become the best car in its class in every category" (Tesla, 2021).

Tesla is all about the future and has moved the schedule forward on amazing, proficient, safe, and efficient modes of transport in this modern age. Tesla not only focuses on the safety of the vehicles but is considerate of their employees, allowing extensive training before they even walk into the factories. Tesla focuses on boosting the economy by providing thousands of jobs and growing their technology as far as they can.

Tesla is different from other auto companies due to their adaptation of technology, having adopted a methodical approach to software and technology available to them. They design their cars similar to how software companies develop apps. They are constantly working on improving and eliminating common car troubles such as oil changes and other issues that tend to cause extra car expenses.

Tesla is also much further ahead than most of the top companies that have been running for the last 100 years in the industry. They have adapted to the changes in technology and simplified the buying process by making it all online. Their eco-friendly approach to the design of their vehicles instantly boosts their popularity in a world that knows the harmful impact that is being made by the transportation industry. They adapted, stayed up-to-date, and assisted with a positive impact on the environment, which is an instant appeal to many people around the world.

Another huge factor to take into consideration is Tesla's recent purchase of $1.5 billion US of Bitcoin, as well as making plans to allow payments via this cryptocurrency. Therefore, if you are interested in Bitcoin, it would be good to consider Tesla—which staked its chances on Bitcoin.

Despite its large growth and great competition, one should consider the following before jumping in and investing in Tesla. They have a reputation of missing deadlines, and the occasional mishap still makes the business volatile, so you should consider several things.

Pros of Investing in Tesla
- Tesla had record-breaking sales and revenue in the last quarter of 2020, having produced 179,757 vehicles (Tesla Investor Relations, 2021).

- They came stunningly close to their prediction of 2020 sales, which in the middle of a global pandemic itself was astounding.
- More opportunities had also opened for Tesla since Joe Biden's victory as America's President, taking office in 2021. Having more companies encouraged to go green sets Tesla well ahead of the curve.

Cons of Investing in Tesla
- It is bizarre to think the CEO himself may give one cause for concern when thinking about investing in Tesla. Elon Musk's fame and controversial tweets have made people considerably doubt whether or not they should invest. Additionally, whether he leaves or stays could cause inevitable damage to the company's reputation.
- Competition against Tesla is on the rise. Depending on how fast these other companies catch up will also have an impact on the future of Tesla and the returns people will get for their stock.

If you would like to invest in Tesla, here are a few steps you can take in order to achieve this. First, you need to open a brokerage account. "A brokerage account is an arrangement in which an investor deposits money with a licensed brokerage firm, who places trades on behalf of the customer" (Brokerage Account, 2021). There are many brokerages available for you to use, but ensure you choose one that is suitable for your financial situation.

You can also consider, as a new investor, hiring a financial advisor. Not only will they help advise you in the current situation with Tesla, but they can also take you through the process step-by-step and give you possible projections of where Tesla is going in the future.

If you think you cannot afford to buy a full share in Tesla, there are multiple other options available, including purchasing fractional shares if you are interested. When opening a brokerage account, you need to know that Tesla's Nasdaq symbol is TSLA. You have the option of purchasing a market order which is the current price of Tesla stock, or you can place a limit order which allows you to set a price limit of what you can afford.

A Peek at NIO

NIO, an automaker in China, is giving Tesla a competitive run for its money. It was created in 2014 and founded in Shanghai. At the moment, NIO stock is only selling in China, and their manufacturing partners are JAC Motors. JAC Motors has been crafting and selling its own range of vehicles across various places around the globe, including Africa, South America, and Europe.

NIOs focus, different from Tesla's, is the ability to swap a dead battery from a vehicle with a new one. This allows vehicles to run longer and faster while cutting down on costs. However, if government subsidies get cut in the future, this might have a major impact on the price advantage it has over Tesla.

NIO trading can be done through tokenized shares, making investments far safer, secure, and easier. You can also open an account and use cryptocurrencies such as Bitcoin and Ether. This gives you an advantage especially considering if you work and trade with cryptocurrencies.

Pros of Investing in NIO
- NIO managed to increase deliveries by over 191% in 2020 in comparison to the prior year (Trefis Team, 2020). This is a good sign of growth within the company, as it shows rapid growth in demand for their vehicles.
- NIO firmly believes they have the production capacity to meet the ever-growing demand, allowing room for more confidence in their abilities as a business.
- NIO had also survived and recovered from a massive cash shortage earlier in 2020, where they could not even pay their employees in time but rather six days late. However, they made a quick recovery through Tencent Holdings through distribution of cash.

- There is a very positive outlook on the future of NIO and its recoveries despite many doubts and reaching the edge of bankruptcy. Therefore, it is easier to believe that this company has the ability to survive and hopefully thrive in the future.

Cons of Investing in NIO
- You could purchase shares far above their deemed value. Therefore, it might be quite a risk. Some analysts view these prices with caution.
- Despite having survived some pretty hard knocks in the company, NIO is still not turning over a profit. This has negative implications and increases the risk, even though there is potential for it to rise and succeed in the future.
- Furthermore, NIO may have come this far, but there is a level of uncertainty about whether it will successfully keep growing or whether it will lose its momentum and fail miserably. All in all, NIO is still a risky investment, and whether you want to purchase stock or not is up to you.

In order to invest in NIO, you will need to decide upon a platform such as Interactive Investor, Hargreaves Lansdown, eToro, or other brokerage accounts before you can proceed. You will need to accurately fill in all your details and do your research on NIO. It is a little less complicated than Tesla, but do keep in mind all the pros and cons before jumping in. Hiring a financial consultant here could also play as an advantage. The average stock price of NIO in March 2021 runs between $40-$45 USD.

Glancing at Apple

Now taking several steps back from the automaker tech industry, it is time to take a peek at the other tech and software companies in the world, including Apple.

Apple was first founded in the garage of Steve Jobs alongside the help of Stephen Wozniak in 1976. Their goal was to design computers that were far more user-friendly than what was available at that point in time. They started selling and slowly but steadily grew in the business world. The Apple II put a shock in the computer industry by adding color and other features like data cassette storage, and it had about $117 million worth of sales by 1980 (Library of Congress, 2011).

Both Wozniak and Jobs left the business at different times in pursuit of other projects. However, due to the struggle Apple faced in 1990-1996, where many believed the company was doomed to bankruptcy, Apple made a final grasp and effort by asking help from Steve Jobs, who was made first interim CEO and then CEO in the 2000s. Steve Jobs made some wise changes to the business, including forming a deal with Microsoft after John Sculley (Apple's former CEO) had turned them down in 1985. Together, they created a version of Microsoft's software that could be used with

Apple products. Steve Jobs also worked on producing other products such as iBook and iTunes, but unfortunately passed away on the 5th of October 2011.

Now more than 40 years later since it was founded, Apple happens to be amongst the most popular and prominent companies in smartphones, computers, and other electronics in the world today. It reached a $2 trillion market cap. With a rough history but amazing recovery, it should definitely be considered as a potential investment. Furthermore, Apple already has a wallet app that you can use for cryptocurrency and also designed a crypto exchange app for the most popular cryptos such as Bitcoin and Bitcoin Cash (Apple Developer Forums, 2020). Therefore, as a tech company, they are also dabbling in cryptocurrency.

Pros of Investing in Apple
- Apple is a favorite in the western technological world. Having an established brand name and flourishing in other software and technology such as the Apple Watch and others, Apple is also focusing on software services of which customers loyally purchase.
- The stabilization of China's economy and tension between America has eased the risk and opened up doors again for Apple to have a relationship restored in China. The number of people in China purchasing Apple products is again on the rise.
- There are new designs and productions ahead that are sure to help boost Apple's competition,

sales, and popularity, including a newly designed TV. If these products flourish, they will be pouring billions more dollars back into the business, which in turn will be very positive for its investors.

Cons of Investing in Apple

- Despite the ease in tension with China, there is still a whirlwind of possibilities, and things could go south with the trade wars that are battling between the countries. Therefore, it is always best to keep a steady eye on both China and America, especially on things that could influence Apple's sales.
- In comparison to its history, Apple's stock has become quite expensive and could be an issue depending upon the amount you can afford to invest and whether you will gain a reasonable return.
- Apple had some recent issues of low revenues that hadn't occurred since 2002. Although this could not be a big issue, one never knows when the tables may turn negatively for Apple. Much like anything, investment is always a risk.

If you decide to jump in and gain your share of this giant tech company, again, a brokerage account is fundamental to start your investing. You can also decide whether or not you want a limit or market order, and then you can make your purchase. Apple is listed as AAPL on the Nasdaq. Remember to keep an eye on your Apple stock and to review it often.

Understanding Adobe

John Warnock and Charles Geschke founded Adobe in 1982. They designed specialized printing software and the PostScript language for printers, and the first products they sold were digital fonts. Warnock and Geschke were both employed by Xerox at the time, and Xerox refused to use their technology. Therefore, they started their own company.

Adobe has been around for 25 years, working on the boundaries of printing and publishing. They focus on the developing and building of effective software tools and have been surviving and thriving.

Pros of Investing in Adobe
- Their applications are ahead of the competition and quite popular in this day and age.
- Adobe's new top-of-the-line technology and developments fulfill the ever-growing demand for software and technological tools.
- Adobe's finances have been solid for a while, increasing their revenue by 14% year-over-year and reporting a 2020 annual revenue of $12.87 billion US (Adobe.com, 2020).

Cons of Investing in Adobe
- There is heavy competition from Microsoft, Apple, Sony, and even free software products

that can turn client's loyalty away as quickly as it comes.

- Any reductions towards the global economy will have an impact on Adobe, considering its market happens to be international.
- Some weak spots have been discovered in some Adobe products which is a major issue as the internet is rife with cybercrime.
- Although, despite all these disadvantages, Adobe has come this far, and its future doesn't look bleak either. With its technology and software development on its side, Adobe is likely to be a strong investment choice.

Much like all the others, it is easy to buy Adobe stock by opening and setting up a brokerage account and purchasing Adobe. Adobe is listed as ADBE on the Nasdaq. If you are in it for the long haul, however, it may be wise to attend their annual meeting. If you intend to sell it quickly, then be sure to set up a stop-loss order.

Considering Cisco

Cisco is a business launched in America, known for products such as networking. Leonard Bosack and Sandy Lerner created and launched Cisco in 1984 and got their start designing routers. Cisco exceeded and grew, surviving way longer than many other competitors in its time and thriving from then.

Chuck Robbins, CEO of Cisco from 2015, swooped in to make some attractive changes within the business in order to grow its market and gain traction again through the alterations of its core assets.

There is also pressure and encouragement for Cisco to seriously consider investing in Bitcoin in order to lead in the next step of technology. As Dan Weiskopf, co-portfolio manager of the Amplify Transformational Data Sharing ETF and member of the Investment Committee at Toroso Investments, said, "Customers in the emerging markets and Asia use Bitcoin as a means to transact. We do not expect large US companies to pay Cisco in Bitcoin, but offering the option of doing so demonstrates Cisco is not limited by US standards and embraces the change that is ubiquitous in the emerging markets and Asia" (Coindesk, 2021).

Pros of Investing in Cisco
- Cisco is advanced in global marketing and grabs opportunities that come their way, thus increasing their odds of survival despite a rough global economy.
- They focus their growth on software and subscription approaches.
- The value of Cisco remains strong, with a high cash flow that allows for higher dividends for its investors.

Cons of Investing in Cisco

- Cisco has some tough competition and needs to stay at the top of its game in order to survive. Any flaw or fluke may cost the company greatly. Even some of Cisco's previous customers have turned into its competitors, for example, Facebook and Alphabet Inc.
- The growth in Cisco has been relatively average in comparison to other businesses. Despite its steady comeback as a business, its slow return may inhibit or affect the dividends investors receive in return.
- Due to the fact that much of Cisco's revenue is global, the purchases and payments take time due to their size and being international. However, with business and income, time is always of the essence and can have a huge impact on revenue.
- It is good to remember that, all in all, Cisco is in the middle of a comeback, and for any large business, it can take time.

Cisco has several stock options that you need to be aware of for its current shareholders and new investors. However, it works similar to the other tech companies mentioned. Do you research and decide whether you want to invest. Cisco is listed as CSCO on the Nasdaq.

On a final chapter note, for many investments, you must be of age and have the money. But some investments may require you to be a citizen of the country in which the business is held. There are other steps to take if you are a foreign investor. Whether it is through a certain application or website, be sure to do the necessary research in order to create a smooth application process for investing wherever you are.

Chapter 8: Bubble or Revolution

A person would probably never have thought that the word "bubble" existed in the financial world, never mind placing "bubble," "revolution," and "finance" in the same sentence. Yet, these are some important concepts to learn, especially in regards to virtual currency and investments.

A Peek at Bubbles

A basic definition of a bubble is when the price of an asset takes a sudden surge beyond its original price value, only in the end to deflate or pop dramatically. This happens when there is a massive hike in a company's stock value which is caused by huge amounts of activities on the market. The asset's price extends way over its actual intrinsic value.

A lot of damage can be caused to the economy due to a financial bubble. It can bankrupt businesses if they are not careful. Whether you have invested before or are just starting out, this is a crucial part of history to understand in order to identify any repetitions of the kind in the future.

Much like anything else, bubbles can take place in various kinds of financial situations.

- Stock market bubbles are the rising of stock values and the sudden deflation.
- Market bubbles happen outside of the equities market and involve matters like real estate or cryptocurrencies.
- Credit bubbles are formed with debt and loans and anything that involves credit.
- Commodity bubbles form in precious metals such as gold or silver.

When a financial bubble is formed, the following steps occur:

1. The start of the bubble normally happens when the items of value are priced exceedingly low.
2. Slowly the prices seem to rise again as more and more investors take interest. In fear of missing out, they jump in, thus letting the price value skyrocket after a certain period of time.
3. The prices reach a peak (like the tip of the mountain). Investors have come to a point in panicking and buying more into the company with distorted beliefs that things are only going to get better. Discretion is replaced with panic buying, and there is a sore loss of logic in the market.

4. The savvy or clever money makers may then start identifying when the bubble is going to burst and take advantage of the overeager investors waiting in line. They start selling their shares and leaving the market before it collapses.
5. The bubble then pops. Normally it takes a particular moment or event to occur. However, prices deflate like a balloon, and much like a balloon's pop, it cannot resurface or recover from its fall.
6. The overeager buyers now start to panic again as they try to sell their shares at whatever price necessary in order to make some minimal recoveries of the damage that has been inflicted.

There are multiple cases of bubble investments or purchases occurring throughout history. One even occurred over Dutch tulips, which caused havoc on the economy.

A classic example of a bubble is the South Sea Bubble. In 1711, the South Sea Company was created under the promise that they would monopolize most trade with the Spanish colonies in South America. Rumors of vast treasures and wealth spread like wildfire thanks to the directors, which led to a surge of investments pouring in. There were also high hopes for this company to have the same success as its predecessor, East India Company. However, as expected of a bubble, the company collapsed, plundering parts of the economy due to the loss.

Another incident occurred in the 1990s, known as the dot-com bubble. This was at the beginning of internet use, and understanding its potential, many investors poured thousands, if not millions, into dot-com companies in hopes of scoring large profits based on the hype. However, not many companies were initially successful with their online stores, and markets crashed in 2002, causing a US recession.

Cryptocurrency Bubbles

Due to the volatile nature of cryptocurrency, it is no wonder that this market is prone to bubbles. There are many means of speculation; some wonder if Bitcoin is one massive bubble, which we'll delve into.

Firstly, due to the lack of regulations in cryptocurrencies and the new but volatile nature, it is hard to pinpoint the peak where bubbles could be formed. The transactions, volatility, and the amount of trading tend to associate or be similar to that of a bubble. The Cboe Volatility Index (2021) tends to point in the opposite direction; they don't indicate that cryptocurrency will be volatile in the immediate 30-day period.

Speculation of Bitcoin

According to the history of Bitcoin, it points to being a bubble, but there is one major exception. Bitcoin started at an exceedingly low trading price. It grew more traction and started to rise. More and more investors grew eager to take their share of the current and new investments. Yet it crashed, devastatingly so. People started to panic and sell their shares with the thoughts of yet again being at a loss. This all follows a bubble pattern. It detoured away from the traditional idea of bubbles when it stabilized instead of reaching ground zero.

Bitcoin could be a bubble because:

- There is nothing tangible about cryptocurrency, and it does not have the support of governments or banks. With traditional currencies, they have at least some form of stability. Crypto, especially Bitcoin, certainly does not.
- Many believe the value comes from the hype and surge of popularity more than anything else and that its value is overinflated.
- Due to the nature of Bitcoin and its global use, there are tax regulations and even complete bans on the use of Bitcoin and cryptocurrency in certain countries.

However, Bitcoin may not be a bubble because:

- Despite its fluctuations, Bitcoin still has a consistent value. Many people, thousands, in fact, accept its value, and thus, this removes part of the uncertainty and instability with Bitcoin.
- Many people have written Bitcoin off as an investment possibility, but there are many others who still invest, despite its reputation. They are willing to take the risk, and at times, it pays off.

One would think this is strange, but because of its volatility, many people actually invest in Bitcoin with the high hopes that the prices skyrocket in a positive direction. This is something that can only truly happen in the cryptocurrency market in comparison to other, more stable forms of investment.

Due to Bitcoin's puzzling behavior, there is great speculation whether Bitcoin was a bubble at all. Although it followed distinct patterns, it did not leave a huge disaster in its wake. This is a common argument people use against those who have a firm and negative belief that Bitcoin is a bubble. Normally when a bubble bursts, the crash is quick and never recovers. Yet Bitcoin has been making a slow and steady rise upwards again.

So it is not possible to give a simple yes or no answer as to whether Bitcoin is one big giant bubble. It had followed some of the trends but also veered away from some. Ultimately, the decision to invest in Bitcoin lies in the hands of the investor.

ICO: A Hotspot for Bubbles

Now with some knowledge of ICO and a basic understanding of bubbles, it is easy to understand how ICOs can indeed be a hotspot for bubbles in the cryptocurrency investment field. With low investment prices that may soar and then suddenly peak, it is a step-by-step catapult into the bubble formula.

However, on the bright side, some people believe that the ICO in and of itself is a bubble that is going to burst. This can occur by allowing only accredited investors to work on the platform and a reduction of scams which will have an overall positive impact, in general.

The biggest issue with ICO is when a huge investment is made on a cryptocurrency idea that hasn't been developed yet. This is much like a company with a goal but no sustainable proof that it will actually be accomplished. So when an idea falls apart, or a scam is uncovered, the bubble bursts and people are left, yet again, without the money and to deal with the damage.

Obviously, that doesn't mean one should not invest in start-up ideas, but one should just be aware of the dangers and risks of doing so. The idea could have a large impact on the economy, and the high risks involved might mean that you won't get a legitimate return.

How the Ethereum Bubble May Burst

In order to make certain purchases or investments on ICO, it is most popular to use Ethers and their smart contracts. The issue here is that Ether is still relatively small, and very few exist.

This also plays a part in the role of a bubble, where the price of Ether skyrockets due to the great demand for investing in ICO and the shortage that Ethereum has. There are a few predictions on how both the ICO and Ethereum bubble are going to burst, and it is a good thing to be prepared.

If people's worst fears occur and Bitcoin's large cryptocurrency empire crumbles, it will not take long before Ethereum (and other altcoins) follow in its footsteps. Bitcoin is the originator, and many people place their trust in the survival of Bitcoin. If Bitcoin shatters that trust, not many will believe in the survival of other coins. Ethereum may have a stronghold and many supporters, but watch people's trust dwindle the moment something as monumental as Bitcoin falls.

Additionally, Ethereum trading has not been getting out of hand; therefore, it hasn't peaked and crashed again. Rather it may be slightly stabilized. So, even if Ethereum was a bubble, it is in a pretty solid place right now. However, if it were to peak and price rise to an exorbitant level, then it would be highly likely to see a crash shortly thereafter.

There is some evidence that points against whether Ethereum is actually a bubble. Economist Harry Dent has stated and believed that Ethereum is by far the most reliable cryptocurrency in the market, having more specialized abilities than Bitcoin (Investopedia, 2021). Ethereum plays on cryptocurrencies' potential. New applications can be built, and Ethereum does not have a limit as it is uncapped.

Therefore, due to Ethereum's potential for growth, people's fears of it being a bubble may be disproven in the long term. However, much like Bitcoin and cryptocurrency in general, there is no surefire way to prove where Ethereum actually stands.

Can One Benefit From a Bubble?

It is indeed possible to benefit immensely from a crypto bubble, yet it is far more of a gamble and a dangerous game to play than any other form of investing. You stand to win majorly, but if you do not get out in time, you will be caught in the market avalanche and lose it all. So bubbles, despite their negative connotations, can play heavily in your favor and your future finances, but playing it wrong could be the biggest risk of all. Therefore, despite its major benefits, do be aware of its major risk.

A Peek at the Cryptocurrency Revolution

Despite all the critics and ups and downs, there are certainly a few technological marvels that are here to stay. "CryptoTradia expects over 95% of these projects to fail. CT focuses on the other 5% that will last and ensure the test of time" (CryptoTradia, 2018). Multiple businesses come and go, and the same could be said for cryptocurrency, yet there are a few things that are here to stay and might help revolutionize cryptocurrency in the future.

Blockchain technology will not be going away any time soon. With its decentralized platforms and websites that are projected to rise in the future, people are looking forward to a more transparent and less controlled way of dealing with things on the web. Most people cannot survive or even work without an internet connection. People feel inhibited by companies that monitor, delete and play a part in every move you make over the web. News is silenced, and biased influence is spread across the internet. It is no wonder people can still feel chained online.

With correct design and software, blockchain technology can be applied practically everywhere. Not only does this inhibit and discourage the constant web hacking and cybercrime, but it takes a step away from the centralized control that a few big companies actually have. Multiple companies are adapting and growing in the background, implementing tokenization and blockchains where possible.

There are a lot of ideas about where cryptocurrencies may go, including using it as a globally adopted manner of paying for items. There are hopes for it to become a legal currency, and eventually, that cryptocurrency might even replace dollars and other old-fashioned forms of currency.

Not all cryptocurrencies are bound to work out. In fact, most of them won't. However, those that survive and thrive in the market may end up becoming the future of finances. One cannot be absolutely certain, but neither can anyone just dismiss the thoughts and intentions behind cryptocurrency any longer. It has lasted for several years, enduring hard crashes and yet, still seen as very risky and volatile. However, if you are looking for a long-term investment, it may actually turn out worth it in the end.

Conclusion

Now drawing to a close, one is only left to wonder, what now? With so many options, opportunities, risks, and truths available, it is now truly the time to start your journey. If you decide to invest and take your chances with cryptocurrencies, remember this—do your research, be wise with what you invest, make a decision, and be patient. It may be easy simply to learn the skills and skirt along the edges of trading and investing. Taking the actual leap—now that is where the true trick lies. If you have never invested before but want to, it is best to start now rather than wait (if your income allows it, of course). The longer you have to learn the craft of investing, the better your chances for success in the long haul.

One can never truly tell or predict where cryptocurrency is going in the future. Many people claim that Bitcoin, the originator of cryptocurrency, is on a pathway of doom. Bitcoin has, however, survived for more than ten years, and more and more evidence is piling up against this theory. No one can be 100% sure, just as no one can claim with absolute confidence that Bitcoin is the future currency of the world, especially considering that Bitcoin is banned in so many countries.

It would be foolish to ignore the investment opportunities that lie before everyone with an internet connection and that blockchain technology is an ingenious and masterful design that may just shape the fate of the internet. Yet, much like anything else, it is rife with problems and risks. There is indeed a dark side to blockchain but there is more freedom without the potentially biased middleman. Decentralized websites may still take over the web, and companies that used to have control may see a dip in their popularity if that time comes.

Countries like Japan have embraced cryptocurrency, while China is forming its own. It is dizzying to think about everything that is happening on the markets and where your best investment opportunities lie. As a beginner, you also want to do your utmost best to avoid the scams and mistakes mentioned. Despite being able to learn from your mistakes, it is wise to learn from the mistakes of others. It would be good to revisit the book often for anything you may have forgotten or tips you would like to brush up on.

Be sure to stay safe on the internet, keeping an eye on your e-wallet, and being careful of empty promises. Remember, if it is too good to be true, then it normally is. Tread carefully, double-check and verify all the information for yourself. Also, ensure you have a thorough and proper understanding of the regulations in your country or any country that you travel to while working with Bitcoin. Some countries are open to accepting it as legal currency, while others may put you in jail if you are not careful.

Keep an eye on the news for anything that may affect your investments but be open-minded as well. Due to cryptocurrencies' volatility, all it could take is one viral tweet at the right place and time that can send cryptos spiraling up or down depending on the message.

Those who are focused on the future and patient enough to roll through the waves with long-term investments tend to gain the rewards. People cannot embrace the get-rich-quick scheme in regards to cryptocurrency because, although it might be possible in some aspects, it is a gamble, and the chances are it won't end up in your favor. Do yourself a favor by immersing yourself in research and getting in contact with other traders and investors who have been playing the game and fighting the battles for longer than you have. Practice paper trading first and do your own research before jumping into any sort of investments.

Beware of the fear of missing out and any other emotions that come into play with investing. Often when investors are trying to get in, this may actually be the time to get out. Looking into the future at what might happen is far better than the empty promises of immediate returns. A business without a goal is like a person without a map wandering in the thick jungle of market competition, hoping to be pointed in the right direction. Make sure your sources of information are trustworthy and remember not to invest money you cannot afford to lose.

Keep in mind there is no perfect strategy when it comes to trading or investing. You will find that as a trader or investor, you will win some battles, and you will lose others—you never know in which order this will come.

Don't allow people or your own emotions and critique to bring you down in a loss. Rather, learn from your mistakes and grow. The more you learn and practice, the fewer losses you will have.

It is highly unlikely that cryptocurrency is going away anytime soon. It may very well be the future of online finance, but there are still multiple flaws in the designs that need to be worked out. The multiple scams and wallet hacks alongside the Ponzi and pyramid schemes create huge dents in this ingenious cryptocurrency and blockchain design. Hopefully, there will be better ways to weed them out, but in time they will always be something to look out for.

Now, with this knowledge, and practical steps to guide you, we leave you with one underlying question. What cryptocurrency actions, both now and in the future, do you want to be a part of?

References

A Quick History of Cryptocurrency in China. (2020, October 8). CryptoVantage. https://www.cryptovantage.com/guides/history-of-crypto-in-china/

A Historical Look at Bitcoin Prices. (n.d.). Trading Education. https://trading-education.com/a-historical-look-at-bitcoin-price-2009-2020

Active vs. Passive Investing: What's Best for You? (2021). Investopedia. https://www.investopedia.com/news/active-vs-passive-investing/#:~:text=Active%20investing%20requires%20a%20hands,funds%20or%20other%20mutual%20funds.

Adobe Systems Incorporated After Big Year – 3 Pros, 3 Cons. (2017, December 28). Nasdaq.com. https://www.nasdaq.com/articles/adobe-systems-incorporated-after-big-year-3-pros-3-cons-2017-12-28

Adobe Reports Record Q4 and Fiscal 2020 Revenue (2020, December 10). Adobe.com.https://news.adobe.com/news/news-details/2020/Adobe-Reports-Record-Q4-and-Fiscal-2020-Revenue-december/default.aspx

Advantages and Disadvantages of Investing - dummies. (2016). Dummies. https://www.dummies.com/personal-

finance/investing/advantages-and-
disadvantages-of-investing/

António Madeira. (2020, September). *OneCoin: A
Deep Dive Into Crypto's Most Notorious Ponzi
Scheme.* Cointelegraph.
https://cointelegraph.com/news/onecoin-a-
deep-dive-into-crypto-s-most-notorious-ponzi-
scheme

Asset Bubbles Through History: The 5 Biggest. (2021).
Investopedia.
https://www.investopedia.com/articles/person
al-finance/062315/five-largest-asset-bubbles-
history.asp

Barker, S. (2019, April 22). *Important Social Media
Marketing Trends That Will Impact Your
Business.* Medium.
https://medium.com/swlh/important-social-
media-marketing-trends-that-will-impact-
your-business-d820bad9db1d

Barton, C. (2020, November 16). *How to Buy NIO
Shares.* Finder UK.
https://www.finder.com/uk/buy-nio-shares

Beware of These Five Bitcoin Scams. (2021).
Investopedia.
https://www.investopedia.com/articles/forex/
042315/beware-these-five-bitcoin-scams.asp

Bitcoin. (2021). Investopedia.
https://www.investopedia.com/terms/b/bitcoi
n.asp

Bitcoin vs. Ethereum: What's the Difference? (2021).
Investopedia.

https://www.investopedia.com/articles/investing/031416/bitcoin-vs-ethereum-driven-different-purposes.asp

Bitcoin's Price History. (2021). Investopedia. https://www.investopedia.com/articles/forex/121815/bitcoins-price-history.asp

Blockchain Explained. (2021). Investopedia. https://www.investopedia.com/terms/b/blockchain.asp#:~:text=Blockchain%20technology%20was%20first%20outlined,could%20not%20be%20tampered%20with.

Brokerage Account. (2021). Investopedia. https://www.investopedia.com/terms/b/brokerageaccount.asp

Cboe Volatility Index (VIX). (2021). Investopedia. https://www.investopedia.com/terms/v/vix.asp#:~:text=The%20Cboe%20Volatility%20Index%2C%20or,market%20when%20making%20investment%20decisions.

China's Digital Currency Electronic Payment Project Reveals the Good and the Bad of Central Bank Digital Currencies. (2020, August 24). Atlantic Council. https://www.atlanticcouncil.org/blogs/new-atlanticist/chinas-digital-currency-electronic-payment-project-reveals-the-good-and-the-bad-of-central-bank-digital-currencies/#:~:text=The%20development%20of%20the%20DCEP%20raises%20fundamental%20questions%20about%20central,an%20alternative%20to%20physical%20cash.

CoinsBank - The Bank of Blockchain Future. (2019). Coinsbank.com. https://coinsbank.com/blog/traders-mistakes-by-beginners

Conklin, A. (2020, February 6). *What are the benefits of cryptocurrency?* Fox Business; Fox Business. https://www.foxbusiness.com/money/what-are-the-benefits-of-cryptocurrency

Conway, L. (2021, January 19). *The 10 Most Important Cryptocurrencies Other Than Bitcoin.* Investopedia. *https://www.investopedia.com/tech/most-important-cryptocurrencies-other-than-bitcoin/*

Cryptocurrency Investing For Dummies Cheat Sheet. (2019). Dummies. https://www.dummies.com/personal-finance/investing/cryptocurrency-investing-for-dummies-cheat-sheet/#:~:text=A%20cryptocurrency%20is%20a%20cross,by%20an%20underlying%20block chain%20technology.

Deep Patel. (2017, December 7). *6 Red Flags of an ICO Scam.* TechCrunch; TechCrunch. https://techcrunch.com/2017/12/07/6-red-flags-of-an-ico-scam/

Electrek. (2021, February 16). *Tesla Competitors Growing in China: NIO, Xpeng, and More.* Electrek. https://electrek.co/2021/02/16/tesla-competitors-growing-in-china-nio-xpeng-and-more/

Enoksen, F. A., Landsnes, Ch. J., Lučivjanská, K., &
    Molnár, P. (2020). Understanding Risk of
    Bubbles in Cryptocurrencies. *Journal of
    Economic Behavior & Organization, 176,* 129–
    144.
    https://doi.org/10.1016/j.jebo.2020.05.005

ET Online. (2017, October 23). *5 Reasons Why You
    Should Go for Cryptocurrency.* The Economic
    Times.
    https://economictimes.indiatimes.com/industr
    y/banking/finance/5-reasons-why-you-should-
    go-for-
    cryptocurrency/articleshow/61184608.cms?fro
    m=mdr

Ethereum. (2021). Investopedia.
    https://www.investopedia.com/terms/e/ethere
    um.asp

Ethereum 101. (2017, March 30). CoinDesk.
    https://www.coindesk.com/learn/ethereum-
    101/what-is-ethereum

February. (2021). *Best Cryptocurrency to Invest in
    February 2021.* Capital.com.
    https://capital.com/best-cryptocurrency-to-
    invest-in-february-2021

Frankel, M. (2020, February 13). *How to Invest
    Money.* The Motley Fool.
    https://www.fool.com/investing/how-to-
    invest/

Frydel, M. (2017, August 18). *The Difference Between
    Investing And Trading Bitcoin.*
    Bitemycoin.com.
    https://bitemycoin.com/trading/the-

difference-between-investing-and-trading-bitcoin/

Gabeci, K. (2021, February 13). *Countries That Bitcoin is Banned in 2021.* Medium. https://medium.datadriveninvestor.com/countries-that-bitcoin-is-banned-in-2021-a29658d4046f?gi=96de1b1ad3bd

Gergely Korpos. (2019, April). *How to Buy Apple Shares? - Handy Guide by Professionals.* BrokerChooser. https://brokerchooser.com/how-to-invest/how-to-buy-apple-shares

Glossary of Cryptocurrency and Blockchain Terms - BitPrime. (2018). BitPrime. https://www.bitprime.co.nz/knowledge-base/glossary-cryptocurrency-blockchain-terms/

Hogan, C. (2017). *4 Things to Know Before Investing in Cryptocurrency.* Chris Hogan; Chris Hogan. https://www.chrishogan360.com/investing/investing-in-cryptocurrency#:~:text=Cryptocurrencies%20are%20digital%20assets%20people,tokens%E2%80%9D%20of%20a%20given%20cryptocurrency.

How To Recognize Bitcoin Ponzi Schemes?. (2020, March 27). NuWireInvestor. https://www.nuwireinvestor.com/can-investors-recognize-bitcoin-ponzi-schemes/

https://facebook.com/shoutharsh. (2020a, November 9). *13 Worse Trading Mistakes Crypto Beginners Make & How to Avoid.* CoinSutra -

Bitcoin Community. https://coinsutra.com/trading-crypto/mistakes/

https://www.facebook.com/thoughtcodotcom. (2019a). *The History of the Man-Made Invention of Money.* ThoughtCo. https://www.thoughtco.com/history-of-money-1992150#:~:text=Metals%20objects%20were%20introduced%20as,of%20coins%20with%20specific%20values.

IB. (2018, December 24). *Is Mining Cryptocurrencies Worth It? The Pros and Cons Before You Start.* Blocks Decoded; Blocks Decoded. https://blocksdecoded.com/mining-cryptocurrency-pros-cons/

Initial Coin Offering (ICO). (2021). Investopedia. https://www.investopedia.com/terms/i/initial-coin-offering-ico.asp#:~:text=An%20initial%20coin%20offering%20(ICO)%20is%20the%20cryptocurrency%20industry's%20equivalent,initial%20public%20offering%20(IPO).&text=Interested%20investors%20can%20buy%20into,token%20issued%20by%20the%20company.

Investing For Dummies Cheat Sheet. (2021, February 22). Dummies. https://www.dummies.com/personal-finance/investing/investing-for-dummies-cheat-sheet/

Is It Possible That Ethereum Is Not in a Bubble? (2021). Investopedia.

https://www.investopedia.com/news/it-possible-ethereum-not-bubble/

Kaspersky. (2021, January 13). *4 Common Cryptocurrency Scams and How to Avoid Them.* Usa.kaspersky.com. https://usa.kaspersky.com/resource-center/definitions/cryptocurrency-scams

Laurent, P. (n.d.). *The Tokenization of Assets Is Disrupting the Financial Industry. Are You Ready?* . https://www2.deloitte.com/content/dam/Deloitte/lu/Documents/financial-services/lu-tokenization-of-assets-disrupting-financial-industry.pdf

Learn About a Bubble in Economics. (2021). Investopedia. https://www.investopedia.com/terms/b/bubble.asp

Listen Money Matters. (2016, December 19). *Investing For Dummies: The No Effort Investment Strategy.* Listen Money Matters. https://www.listenmoneymatters.com/investing-for-dummies/

Loona Jarvloo. (2020, February 6). *Cryptocurrency Regulations Around the World.* ComplyAdvantage. https://complyadvantage.com/blog/cryptocurrency-regulations-around-world/

Lutkevich, B. (2017). *Tokenization.* TechTarget. https://searchsecurity.techtarget.com/definition/tokenization#:~:text=Tokenization%2C%20

which%20seeks%20to%20minimize,with%20i
ndustry%20standards%20and%20government

M, L. (2020, October). *Is Bitcoin A Bubble: The Great Bitcoin Bubble Burst*. BitDegree.org. https://www.bitdegree.org/crypto/tutorials/is-bitcoin-a-bubble

Marshall, A. (2017, March 7). *ICO, Explained*. Cointelegraph. https://cointelegraph.com/explained/ico-explained

Niklas Goeke. (2016, February 22). *The Intelligent Investor*. Four Minute Books; Niklas Goeke. https://fourminutebooks.com/the-intelligent-investor-summary/

Online Shopping Statistics You Need to Know in 2021. (2019, November 6). OptinMonster. https://optinmonster.com/online-shopping-statistics/#:~:text=So%20far%2C%2069%25%20of%20Americans,the%20world%20understa nd%20the%20benefits

Payment Tokenization Explained. (2014). Square. https://squareup.com/us/en/townsquare/what-does-tokenization-actually-mean

Ponzi Schemes. (2014). Acfe.com. https://www.acfe.com/ponzi-schemes.aspx

Powers, B. (2020, December 16). *New to Bitcoin? Stay Safe and Avoid These Common Scams*. CoinDesk. https://www.coindesk.com/new-to-bitcoin-stay-safe-and-avoid-these-common-scams

Praveen Jayachandran. (2017, May 31). *The Difference Between Public and Private Blockchain* - IBM Blockchain Blog. https://www.ibm.com/blogs/blockchain/2017/ 05/the-difference-between-public-and-private-blockchain/

Pros and Cons of Investing in Bitcoin, Will It Be a Millionaire Maker? (2021). Trading-Education.com. https://trading-education.com/pros-and-cons-of-investing-in-bitcoin-will-it-be-a-millionaire-maker

Pros and Cons of Investing in Ethereum, Will It Be a Millionaire Maker? | Trading Education. (2021). Trading-Education.com. https://trading-education.com/pros-and-cons-of-investing-in-ethereum-will-it-be-a-millionaire-maker

What is a Pyramid Scheme? (2021). Investopedia. https://www.investopedia.com/insights/what-is-a-pyramid-scheme/

Regulation of Cryptocurrency Around the World. (2014). Loc.gov. https://www.loc.gov/law/help/cryptocurrency /world-survey.php

Rostyslav Demush. (2020, November 23). *The Dark Side of The Blockchain: ICOs and the Ethereum Bubble.* Perfectial. https://perfectial.com/blog/ico-and-ethereum-bubble/

Royal, J. (2018, January 11). *What Is Cryptocurrency? Here's What You Should Know.* NerdWallet.

https://www.nerdwallet.com/article/investing/cryptocurrency-7-things-to-know

Royal, J. (2021, February 23). *9 best investments in 2021.* Bankrate.com. https://www.bankrate.com/investing/best-investments/

Simply Explained. (2017). How does a Blockchain Work - Simply Explained [YouTube Video]. https://www.youtube.com/watch?v=SSo_EIwHSd4

Sneha Kulkarni. (2021, February 27). *Why Bitcoin the Cryptocurrency is Banned in Some Countries.* Goodreturns. https://www.goodreturns.in/classroom/why-cryptocurrencies-bitcoin-are-banned-in-some-countries-india-saudi-arabia-qatar-1208098.html

Sraders, A. (2020, February 11). *Pay Attention to These 7 Bitcoin Scams.* The Street Investing. https://www.thestreet.com/investing/bitcoin-scams-14640202

Stieglitz, J. (2017, September 12). *Encryption: Pros and Cons.* Blog; Imperva. https://www.imperva.com/blog/encryption-pros-and-cons/

Tamal Nandi. (2020, May 6). *Crypto Scams Are on the Rise: 5 Ways to Avoid Them.* Mint. https://www.livemint.com/technology/tech-news/crypto-scams-are-on-the-rise-5-ways-to-avoid-them-11588775510857.html

Team Luno. (2018, September 26). *How Do Financial Bubbles Really Work?* Medium. https://medium.com/swlh/how-do-financial-bubbles-really-work-9d2ffca8de7

Tesla Q4 2020 Vehicle Production & Deliveries. (2021, January 2). Tesla Investor Relations. https://ir.tesla.com/press-release/tesla-q4-2020-vehicle-production-deliveries

The Decentralized Web. (2020, January 2). MIT Digital Currency Initiative. https://dci.mit.edu/decentralizedweb

The History Of Adobe. (2021). Google.com. https://sites.google.com/site/theadobeproject/home/history/history

The Science Behind Exploding Cell Phones. (2021). Towerfast.com. https://towerfast.com/press/post/the-science-behind-exploding-cell-phones#:~:text=Recently%2C%20Samsung%20recalled%20its%20Galaxy,are%20not%20only%20Samsung's%20problem.

Tokenization. (2020, February 17). CoinGeek. https://coingeek.com/bitcoin101/what-is-tokenization/

Top 9 Advantages of Cryptocurrency as a Financial Medium. (2018, January 9). Finjan Blog. https://blog.finjan.com/advantages-of-cryptocurrency/

Using Paper Trading to Practice Day Trading. (2021). Investopedia. https://www.investopedia.com/day-trading/how-practice-day-trading/#:~:text=Pros%20of%20Paper%20Trading,-Starting%20out%20with&text=First%2C%20you%20have%20no%20risk,help%20create%20a%20winning%20strategy.

Vincent, D. (2020, September 24). *One Day Everyone Will Use China's Digital Currency.* BBC News. https://www.bbc.com/news/business-54261382

Voigt, K. (2019, June 14). *How to Buy Bitcoin.* NerdWallet. https://www.nerdwallet.com/article/investing/how-to-invest-in-bitcoin

Volt Technology. (2019, May 30). *Top 5 Disadvantages Of Cryptocurrency.* Medium. https://medium.com/the-capital/top-5-disadvantages-of-cryptocurrency-925d6679195d

Weliver, D. (2019, December 12). *7 Easy Ways To Start Investing With Little Money.* Money Under 30. https://www.moneyunder30.com/start-investing-with-little-money

What Are the Different Types of Investments? (2021). Commsec.com.au. https://www.commsec.com.au/education/learn/investing-basics/what-are-the-different-types-of-investments.html

What is Ethereum? (2021). Ethereum.org. https://ethereum.org/en/what-is-ethereum/

What is Tesla? (2017, March 27). Tech Monitor. https://techmonitor.ai/what-is/what-is-tesla-4939228

When Did We Start Using Money? (2017, March 7). Economy. https://www.ecnmy.org/learn/your-money/past-present-and-future/when-did-we-start-using-money/?gclid=CjoKCQiA4feBBhC9ARIsABp_nbWLTQNgJ5sRUiQZw5749_xwYp7kmH-TF98ZAY-pNzmjnx3GK_W_AjEaAv9SEALw_wcB

Whittaker, M. (2021). *Should You Buy Apple (AAPL) Stock?* U.S. News & World Report. https://money.usnews.com/investing/stock-market-news/articles/pros-and-cons-to-buying-apple-aapl-stock

Weiskopf, D. (2021, March 3). *Why Cisco Should Buy Bitcoin.* Coindesk.com. https://www.coindesk.com/why-cisco-should-buy-bitcoin

Why Ethereum's Bubble May Not Have Burst Yet. (2021, January 12). Nasdaq.com. https://www.nasdaq.com/articles/why-ethereums-bubble-may-not-have-burst-yet-2021-01-12

Wikipedia Contributors. (2021, March 5). *Legality of Bitcoin by Country or Territory.* Wikipedia; Wikimedia Foundation. https://en.wikipedia.org/wiki/Legality_of_bitcoin_by_country_or_territory

Wikipedia Contributors. (2021, March 7). *History of Bitcoin.* Wikipedia; Wikimedia Foundation.

https://en.wikipedia.org/wiki/History_of_bitc
oin

Zoë Corbyn. (2018a, September 8). *Decentralisation: The Next Big Step for the World Wide Web.* The Guardian; The Guardian. https://www.theguardian.com/technology/201 8/sep/08/decentralisation-next-big-step-for-the-world-wide-web-dweb-data-internet-censorship-brewster-kahle